Praise for You Don't Have to Do It Alone

"I worked with one of the authors of this book on a major programme of reform. When we started I wasn't sure these ideas for involving people would work. But they did. The whole thing was a huge success and I was proud of it. The book is an easy read and shows a wise understanding of human nature. I commend it."

—Lord Wilson of Dinton, Master of Emmanuel College, Cambridge, Former Cabinet Secretary and Head of the UK Home Civil Service

"When you are doing something big, intentional design and high involvement strategies lead to great results. Dick, Emily, Julie, and Jake's book gives us practical guidance on how to get such results. These ideas can be used equally by project managers, line managers, union leaders, community organizers, and even by family members."

—Jan Mears, Human Resources Director, Global Supply Chain, Kraft Foods

"An extraordinarily useful, user-friendly, and wise guide for creating the conditions for true participation. In the current climate, we keep forgetting that people only support what they create. Here is easy guidance for how to engage people so that they genuinely support change."

—Margaret J. Wheatley, author, *Leadership and the New Science, Turning to One Another, A Simpler Way*

"*You Don't Have to Do It Alone* is a fresh, optimistic, practical guide to involving others. Chock full of examples, tools, and checklists, it enables you to involve others in an organized and thoughtful manner. The rich wisdom contained within will appeal to novice and experienced leaders as they apply its lessons in religious organizations, community groups, businesses, and even their own families! This book promises that you don't have to do it alone and delivers on its promise in a most empowering manner."

—Philip Mirci, Ph.D., Director, Student and Family Advocacy for San Bernardino County Superintendent of Schools

"*You Don't Have to Do It Alone* comes at a perfect time for our organization and is a marvelous companion to *Terms of Engagement*. As we work toward our vision—Better Health, Best in Healthcare—we know there will be profound change in how care is delivered, how individuals and communities interact with the health system, and how change is led and implemented. We now have a clear, pragmatic, and workable framework for moving forward by dealing with our fears and focusing on our hopes."

—Geoffrey Crampton, Vice President, Human Resources & Organization Development, Fraser Health Authority, Surrey, Canada

"You know how strategic plans sometimes gather dust? Not so in our organization. We followed the steps in *You Don't Have to Do It Alone*, and that helped us form stronger partnerships with students, parents, teachers, universities, and the people who fund us. We are refocused and recommitted to our mission, and we've developed forward thinking action plans that we are now implementing."

—Arnold Aprill, Exe   ) in Education

"Involving others is fundamental to th   multitude of useful and practical insights to help us   irst class tool, especially for those of us working with   of Shrewsbury

"*You Don't Have to Do It Alone* is one of the clearest books I have ever read. There isn't one wasted sentence. Human resource professionals, team leaders, supervisors, and managers will all find something here to make them more effective. I particularly like the tools and templates that accompany each major concept. They are easy to use and can be applied in many different settings."

—Ken Goldstein, Director of Management Development, Mattel, Inc.

"*You Don't Have to Do It Alone* inspires you to take the risk and involve others. Its practical approach is so easy to follow and I had never before realized the power of invitations. As I read each chapter, I was left with a feeling of wanting to 'have a go.' The checklists are superb once your project is underway. This is an invaluable resource for any school community."

—Helen McKay, Head Teacher, St. Michael's Church of England Primary School, Lichfield

"An indispensable, practical guide on how to successfully introduce involvement practices in the workplace. A 'must read' if you want to increase the commitment and engagement levels of your people."

—Anne Gill, Vice President, Human Resources, Avon Cosmetics, Ltd.

"This book is so smooth it's hard to imagine that four people wrote it. The authors lived what they are writing about—they got something wonderful done by involving each other. This is a practical book. It provides numerous stories and examples from multiple walks of life. The concepts come alive. They help me see new ways to involve others. I am using the 'How Do I Keep People Involved' chapter right now to work through a low energy period people are experiencing in a transformation project I am leading. I thank you for an easy-to-read, action-oriented presentation about when, why, and how to involve others to get things done."

—Carl McAulay, Vice President, Human Resources, Unocal Corporation

"*You Don't Have to Do It Alone* will be an important resource for everyone who knows the value of teamwork but worries about the difficulties involved in establishing it. It will be particularly helpful in the not-for-profit sector, where staff are expected to involve and consult but haven't always had the practical tools to help them put those fine words into practice. Now they do."

—Simon Bottery, Communications Director, Citizens Advice Bureau, United Kingdom

"The book makes a strong case for involving others to solve many organizational problems. With it you can confidently reach out to others for help and get things done in families, communities, and all dimensions of life."

—Dr. Rogelio A. Martinez H., Organizational Transformation Consultant and Professor, Tecnológico de Monterrey, EGADE, Monterrey, N. L., Mexico

"The Axelrods, Beedon, and Jacobs present a powerful challenge to the way many leaders 'get things done.' If the ideas in the book were adopted wholesale by the leadership community, we would waste a lot less energy on implementing change programs that will never fulfill their promise."

—Helen Bevan, Director of Innovation & Knowledge, NHS Modernisation Agency, Leicester, England

"*You Don't Have to Do It Alone* is a book you will want to keep on your desk and turn to often. The authors weave together a bit of Maslow in basic human understanding with John Lockeian higher ideals, wrapped in a healthy dose of Tom Sawyer practicality. With this book, you will get your fence painted!"

—Ron Thomas, Executive Director, Northeastern Illinois Planning Commission

You Don't Have to Do It Alone

You Don't Have to Do It Alone

How to Involve Others to Get Things Done

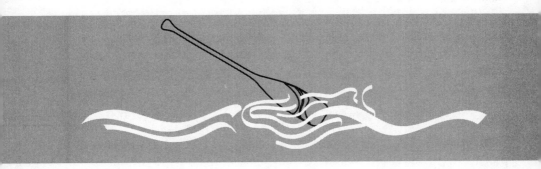

Richard H. Axelrod
Emily M. Axelrod
Julie Beedon
Robert W. Jacobs

BERRETT-KOEHLER PUBLISHERS, INC.
San Francisco

Berrett-Koehler Publishers, Inc.
235 Montgomery Street, Suite 650
San Francisco, CA 94104-2916
Tel: (415) 288-0260   Fax: (415) 362-2512   www.bkconnection.com

Ordering Information

Quantity sales. Special discounts are available on quantity purchases by corporations, associations, and others. For details, contact the "Special Sales Department" at the Berrett-Koehler address above.
Individual sales. Berrett-Koehler publications are available through most bookstores. They can also be ordered directly from Berrett-Koehler: Tel: (800) 929-2929; Fax: (802) 864-7626; www.bkconnection.com
Orders for college textbook/course adoption use. Please contact Berrett-Koehler: Tel: (800) 929-2929; Fax: (802) 864-7626.
Orders by U.S. trade bookstores and wholesalers. Please contact Publishers Group West, 1700 Fourth Street, Berkeley, CA 94710. Tel: (510) 528-1444; Fax (510) 528-3444.

Berrett-Koehler and the BK logo are registered trademarks of Berrett-Koehler Publishers, Inc.

Printed in the United States of America

Berrett-Koehler books are printed on long-lasting acid-free paper. When it is available, we choose paper that has been manufactured by environmentally responsible processes. These may include using trees grown in sustainable forests, incorporating recycled paper, minimizing chlorine in bleaching, or recycling the energy produced at the paper mill.

Library of Congress Cataloging-in-Publication Data

You don't have to do it alone : how to involve others to get things done / Richard H. Axelrod . . . [et al.].
    p. cm.
    Includes index.
    ISBN 1-57675-278-X
    1. Social groups. 2. Collective behavior. 3. Group decision making. I. Axelrod, Richard H., 1943-

HM716.Y68 2004
302.3—dc22   2004046254

First Edition
08 07 06 05 04   10 9 8 7 6 5 4 3 2 1
Compositor/production service: Shepherd, Inc.

To Our Children and Grandchildren:
For the joy and inspiration you bring to our lives

David Boushee Axelrod, Kirk Alan Beedon, Livia Eve Beedon, Aaron Matthew Jacobs, Alison Marie Jacobs, Heather Axelrod Oliver, Timothy James Oliver, Zachary James Oliver, Andrew Isaac Oliver

CONTENTS

PREFACE

The question is not "whether to involve or not to involve." The question is how to do it well.

People work with others to get things done from the time they get up in the morning until the time they go to bed. They get kids off to school, help neighbors clear their driveways, build roads, make dinner, sit on village boards, and lead Girl Scout meetings.

But what do we mean by involvement? Our definition is simple. It is working with others to get things done. When involvement goes well, people work together to make something happen. They contribute their time, their energy, their money, their brains, and their brawn. When the work is complete, they experience the satisfaction that can only come from working with others to achieve a common goal. When involvement goes badly, tasks don't get done. People end up feeling as if they were the only ones who cared about the outcome. They feel that their time and talents were wasted, their voices not heard, and their contribution ignored.

Ineffective involvement wastes time and requires more work than if you do it yourself, all of which leads to not getting work done. Effective involvement can accelerate progress, prevent conflicts, provide creative ideas, and generate support.

We wrote this book for people for whom time is of the essence; people who want others involved in a straightforward, no-nonsense way; people who can't afford to backtrack because things weren't done well in the first place.

Our goal in writing this book is to take the mystery out of effective involvement. When involvement goes well, it almost seems magical. But effective involvement is not magic. Effective involvement depends on the questions you ask and how you answer them. By the time you have completed this book, you will have learned an effective way of involving others.

This book's lessons apply to any kind of involvement. You might need to get things done at home when planning a family vacation or moving to a new house. Or you may be trying to gather support for a community initiative such as the local blood drive, a garage sale, or combating drunk driving. You may be tackling projects at work such as preparing for an important presentation, working with customers and suppliers to reduce cycle time, or figuring out how your crew will meet the daily production schedule. This book's lessons apply whenever and wherever you involve others.

In writing this book, we aimed to practice what we preach. Any one of us could have written this book alone. But we knew that writing it together would make the book decidedly better. Why is that? Because our involvement experiences are so varied. We have coached swimming teams, served in the military, worked in ice cream factories, lived around the world, consulted to local dentist offices, schools, governments, and major corporations. This rich tapestry of experiences brought depth and creativity to *You Don't Have to Do It Alone*. Here are some of the life experiences that shaped our thinking.

Dick Axelrod's early experiences working on the line in his father's model airplane factory taught him that no matter where you work in the organization, people have ideas about how to make it better. As an army officer in Korea, he learned that rank gives you authority to force people to do things, but when people are included in the plans, they not only do things willingly, they improve the plan. His work with self-directed work teams at General Foods taught him how productive people can be when they are allowed to manage their own work. He received an MBA from the University of Chicago, where he learned how to manage within a traditional hierarchical organization. Nevertheless, he has spent the bulk of his career creating egalitarian work systems.

Emily Axelrod brings Southern wit and spirit to her work with organizations and family businesses. She coached swimming at the University of Illinois where she learned that even in individual sports such as swimming, involvement matters. She has two master's degrees, one in education from the University of North Carolina and one in social work from Loyola University. Her work in education taught her how family involvement is key to a child's success in school. As a family therapist, working with families in crisis, she learned the importance of including the whole family in resolving issues, not just the "identified patient." Emily currently serves on the Board of Directors of the Illinois Chapter of the National Association of Social Workers where she works with others to address social policy for the State of Illinois.

With a father in the Royal Navy, Julie Beedon was raised in various locations around the United Kingdom and in Singapore, where she learned about living and working in different cultures. She ultimately earned degrees in mathematics and social science through the UK's Open University. Julie combines the precision of a mathematician and the insight of an anthropologist in her work. Her extensive knowledge of the public sector taught her how involvement works in highly political, complex, bureaucratic systems. She has a multitude of experiences in involvement within voluntary organizations and currently runs the Youth Group for a United Benefice in the Lichfield Diocese of the Anglican Church. People participate in voluntary organizations because they want to, not because they have to. From these experiences Julie learned the importance of the invitation.

Robert "Jake" Jacobs first learned about involvement on the basketball courts of northwest Ohio. He realized early on that the best teams involved each player so that they could all make their unique contributions. In the product packaging room at an ice cream novelty manufacturing plant at the age of eighteen, he learned how mindless life can be when you are uninvolved. A stint at tending bar was a great teacher about involving others. The camaraderie of the staff and patrons in creating a great shared experience proved to be a key to the bar's success. After earning a master's degree in organization development, Jake has devoted his life to helping organizations create their future faster. His basic working theory: Wouldn't it be better to be living in your preferred future, now?

We are all pioneers in the field of large group interventions (LGIs), an involvement process that takes participation to the max. In LGIs, hundreds, sometimes even thousands of people create strategic plans, redesign organizations, and shift cultures. Julie Beedon is seen as the leading LGI authority in the UK, while Jake Jacobs and Dick and Emily Axelrod are internationally recognized experts in LGI. Jake helped to develop an LGI called Real Time Strategic Change, and Dick and Emily Axelrod are creators of The Conference Model®.

In writing this book, we have taken many of our insights from working with large groups and applied them to involving people in groups big and small. The steps we outline in this book work with a group of five or five thousand.

This book has been in development in one form or another for over three years. One of its earlier incarnations had us meeting with a group of over thirty colleagues to create a field book. None of us who were there will ever forget that day. It was September 11, 2001. Even though we did not write the field guide we started out to write, the book you have in your hands today has its roots in these earlier experiences.

Our writing process went like this. First we interviewed effective involvers we knew to find out the questions they had about involving others. These became the key questions we built the book around. Then we set about answering these questions. We would then brainstorm our answers. Then one of us would take responsibility for writing the chapter, supported by a "writing buddy." After the chapter was drafted, we would all read and comment on it. We then shared the draft with our "advisory group" and incorporated their comments into the final manuscript.

There were times when each of us thought that it would be simpler to write this book alone. Involving so many people demanded a lot of time and effort. But in the end, it was worth it. The support we received from everyone made our writing easier. We ended up being more creative than we could have been on our own. And involving others made our points clearer.

We want to thank the following people who worked with us to create this book and whose thoughtfulness and insights brought our manuscript to life.

Steve Piersanti, our publisher, colleague, and friend, saw the germ of an idea and nurtured it from its very inception until its final product.

"Magical" Mark Levy was our writing coach. Most people would throw up their hands in horror when presented with the idea of coaching four authors. Mark rolled up his sleeves and approached the project with glee. Mark made writing fun as he made us all better writers.

We had other teachers along the way. Richard Ogle taught us about reader-writer dialogues and Laura Bonnazoli taught us how to avoid "kitchen drawer paragraphs."

Our advisory group, made up of effective involvers from industry, government, and the not-for-profit sectors, was with us from almost the very beginning. They helped us to formulate the five questions that are at the core of this book and determine the content of the chapters, and they read many versions of the manuscripts. Thanks to Jan Mears, Amanda Fleming, Helen MacKay, Keith Smith, and Sharon Schacter. Your insightful feedback was always useful.

There were others who read the final manuscript and whose comments were very important in transforming our original manuscript into the book it is today. Thanks to Charles Dorris, Scott Gassman, Linda Klatt, Sue Talbot, Leif Ulstrup, Nancy Voss, Rosemarie Barbeau, Gary Hochman, and

Nancy Aronson. You read our manuscript with a critical eye and in doing so made it better.

To the folks who were with us in Chelsea, Michigan, on September 11, 2001, we will always know who we were with on that fateful day: Francine Alexander, Nancy Aronson, Beverly Arsht, Rosi Barbeau, Laura Bonazzoli, Paul Cox, Leslie DePol, Becky DeStefano, June Gunter, Karin Hedenstrom, Kay L. Hubbard, Barry Johnson, Susan Law, Sam Magill, Linda McFadden, Richard Ogle, Julian Simcox, Steve Treacy, and Nancy Voss. A special thank you goes to Anne Brooks, who makes things happen, even when they seem impossible.

Finally, a big thanks to our families for putting up with our craziness during the writing process.

Richard H. Axelrod, Emily M. Axelrod,
Julie Beedon, Robert W. Jacobs

INTRODUCTION

Everyone loves involvement in the abstract. Involving others is a great idea and being involved has universal appeal. No matter how much we love the involvement ideal, when it comes down to involving others or being involved, our fears get in the way.

Involvers worry about whom to include and how to include them. When we are the ones who are asked to participate, we have another set of concerns. We want our voices to be heard and we want our ideas to be accepted. We want to experience the satisfaction that occurs when we pull together to make something happen.

Fears and Hopes Around Involvement

What do we worry about? We worry about the time it takes to involve others. We worry about the hassle that occurs when we have to incorporate other points of view. We worry about loss of control. And we worry about failure.

Let's take a look at these fears from two perspectives—that of the involver and that of the person asked to be involved.

It will take too long. *The involver fears:* Involving others will delay getting things done, causing me to miss important deadlines. *The involved person fears:* If I get involved, it will take a lot of time away from my day-to-day work, leaving me with more work to do.

It's going to require more effort. *The involver fears:* It's going to take a lot of work to include others. I will have to bring them up to speed, figure out who needs to be involved, and then work through their differing opinions of what needs to be done. *The involved person fears:* If I get involved, I'm going to have to convince my boss what needs to be done, and I'm not sure he's interested. Besides, while I'm doing that, my own work won't get done. It all seems to be more trouble than it's worth.

I will lose control. *The involver fears:* Bringing people together means that I will not be able to predict the outcome. If I do it myself, I might not have the right answer, but at least it's an answer I can live with. It's just easier to do it myself. *The involved person fears:* If I become involved, it means I'm going to have to consider others' opinions. I don't want to make compromises when I know what needs to be done.

I will fail. *The involver fears:* When it's all said and done, I'm the one who is responsible. If we fail, no one will blame them. It will all come back to me. I'm not sure that others feel the same sense of ownership that I do. *The involved person fears:* If I get involved, I'm going to have to live with what we decide. I'm not sure that others care as much as I do. Will we suggest ideas that make things worse instead of better? Will we be worse off in the end?

If these fears ruled the day, involvement would never happen. But opposite these fears reside four hopes. What kind of hopes? The hope that by involving others time will be saved, the work will be made easier, new ideas will emerge, and we will create allies to support our work.

Now let's look at our hopes from both perspectives.

The work will get done faster. *The involver hopes:* If I involve others, there will be more people to do the work. I won't have to spend late nights and weekends organizing the garage sale or working on a presentation for my boss. If I involve others, they will be able to take over some of what I do. That will free up my time so that I can do the things that I'm best at doing, where I can make a real contribution. *The involved person hopes:* By getting involved I hope that I will be helpful. I hope that by working with others I will help the job get done sooner. I hope that my contribution will make things go faster.

The job will be easier. *The involver hopes:* Instead of doing everything myself there will be others to call on to do the heavy lifting. Knowing that others are there to do the work will help me sleep at night. *The involved person hopes:* I hope that by joining this group the work will go more smoothly. I hope to pull my weight. I want to have fun. I hope that more hands will make light work.

Better ideas will develop. *The involver hopes:* If I give up some control, I hope I get better ideas in return. My fondest hope in involving others is that we will come up with new and better ways to do the job—ideas that take a fresh look at old problems, ideas that provide solutions I couldn't see because I've worked on the problem for too long. *The involved person hopes:* By getting involved I hope that I will make a contribution. I hope to help generate fresh ideas so that we come up with some new solutions to old problems.

There will be other people to support me. *The involver hopes:* What I want most are allies, people to support my efforts, people to spread the word and encourage others to join. I want to know that there are others besides myself who are willing to work hard toward achieving the goal. When I'm feeling discouraged, having allies gives me the courage to move on. *The involved person hopes:* I hope that by joining this group I will make new allies. I hope that instead of feeling that I have to do everything myself, there will be people to help me along the way.

Building a Foundation

Dealing successfully with hopes and fears requires a solid foundation.

The Japanese bullet train zooms over 200 miles an hour as it makes its way from Tokyo to Kyoto. But in the United States, similar trains barely reach speeds of 100 miles an hour. What's the difference? The foundation—the tracks they sit on. American railroads are built on tracks that were designed for steam locomotives in the nineteenth century. Japanese lines feature high-tech tracks specifically built to accommodate the ultra-fast bullet train.

Fearing a horrendous accident, we would never think of running the bullet train in the United States at 200 miles an hour. But when the track bed is safe, we don't give these speeds a second thought.

By fully acknowledging our hopes and fears, we create a solid foundation for involving others. When we build our foundation with our fears in mind, we are aware of them, but we don't let our fears prevent us from moving forward. In the same way, while our hopes inspire us to action, we are not Pollyannaish about the task before us.

The Five Questions

This book is organized around a series of five questions that help us deal with our hopes and fears. When answered, these questions help us build a solid foundation for involving others. These five questions are asked by effective involvers whenever they tackle a new challenge. Answering these questions will allow you to build a safe track bed, one that allows you to move swiftly to your destination. The questions are:

- What kind of involvement is needed?
- How do I know whom to include?
- How do I invite people to become involved?
- How do I keep people involved?
- How do I finish the job?

We devote a chapter to showing you how to answer each question whenever you take on new work. We also offer a chapter called "Meetings: The Involvement Edge" that provides a blueprint for designing high-involvement meetings. A concluding chapter, "Where to Start," provides options for where to begin. There are also a reference set of checklists and some ideas for further learning.

What kind of challenges do effective involvers tackle? It could mean solving a problem at work that has been bugging you for months. It could mean saving your company millions of dollars. It could mean launching a community movement to improve your schools or the local health care system. It might even mean drawing on the ideas and energies of thousands of citizens to decide the future of the World Trade Center site in New York City.

Our approach has been tested for the past ten years in organizations such as Boeing, Marriott, and the Cabinet Office of the British Government. These are no-nonsense organizations where time is of the essence, resources like money and talent are precious, and the pressures to perform are enormous. They are also subject to intense scrutiny by many stakeholders, from corporate shareholders and employees to civic groups and ordinary citizens. The plans such organizations develop and the means they use to carry them out *must* be effective; if they are not, the repercussions may be enormous. These organizations have learned that effective involvement is the key to making smart decisions and making them work better. We predict that you will discover this, too.

How do we know these are the right questions? Effective involvers told us so. We asked some of the most productive, creative, and resourceful people we know to walk us through their own techniques for organizing and managing their work. The structure of the book grew out of what they told us. These same effective involvers also read the chapters as they were written and helped us shape the contents to be as useful and practical as possible.

Taken together, the steps in *You Don't Have to Do It Alone* provide you with the tools for creating organizational energy—the kind of energy that can only come when we involve others to get things done. We begin to involve others when we ask ourselves the first question, "What kind of involvement is needed?" Your journey toward successful involvement begins on the next page.

Chapter 1

WHAT KIND OF INVOLVEMENT IS NEEDED?

A few years ago, Jake was faced with a challenging project. A friend had given him his first puppy, a black Labrador retriever. His family already had dogs; his daughter and son each had one. But Theo (named after jazz great Thelonius Monk) was Jake's first, and that made him responsible for everything from feeding and training the puppy to taking him outside in the middle of the night when nature called.

Theo proved to be an active little guy. His idea of fun included activities like chewing on someone's sandal and polishing off a whole chicken left unguarded on a kitchen counter.

After a few days of this, Jake's wife helped him get clear that more involvement was needed. "You have three choices, honey," she patiently explained. "Theo can clean up his act, or you can find him another home."

"What's the third choice?" Jake wondered.

"*You* can find a new home. Do I make myself clear?"

"Crystal."

Jake's work was cut out for him. The kids already considered Theo part of the family—to say nothing about Jake's growing attachment to the pup. But Theo needed to behave better if the Jacobs' happy home was to remain intact.

Jake trying to get the job done alone was not the ticket. Different people with different kinds of involvement were needed. First came the instructor at an obedience class. Next came the kids. Someone had to partner with Theo on his homework when Jake was out of town on business. Theo had to pitch in and do his fair share. He had to learn that sandals were for people's feet, not dogs' mouths, and that his food was in a bowl on the floor, not on a tray on the counter. Even Jake's wife had to reluctantly get involved so the pupil received consistent rewards and corrections.

Jake was confident of success if everyone pulled together. And they did.

Today when Theo and Jake take walks around town, people comment on what a good dog he is. Most days Theo visits Jake's office, where he's become a company mascot. It's even been more than a year since he ate the chicken that was left unattended in the kitchen one day!

By involving others, Jake achieved both of his goals: a four-legged friend for life and a reasonably contented wife.

Is Doing It Alone Your Best Answer?

In Jake's situation, it was clear he needed to involve others. But it's not often such a clear-cut decision. Involving other people takes time. There's an inherent "hassle factor" when you get more cooks in the kitchen. How will it impact the quality of the work you do? Are you going to have to make too many concessions to keep people satisfied that their voices are being heard? Is your invitation for others to get involved the first step down a slippery slope where every decision becomes a never-ending debate? Your track record of including others may have left a bad taste in your mouth.

Given these possible headaches, it's important to decide whether it makes sense to involve others before getting clear on what kind of involvement you might need. We recommend you start with a tool we call the *Return on Involvement Assessment Tool*. It can help you decide from the get-go whether to involve other people in what you're up to.

ROI is business shorthand for *return on investment*. It's a standard way of assessing the potential value of a financial transaction. The ROI calculation answers the question, "Is this work worthwhile from a financial perspective?" Initiatives with higher returns on investment are allocated time, money, and other resources. Initiatives with lower ROIs get put on hold or are scrapped.

This traditional definition of ROI doesn't deal with the additional question, "Does it make sense to involve others in this work?" To answer that question, effective involvers supplement the traditional return on investment analysis with a *return on involvement* analysis. This second type of ROI focuses on whether an involvement-based approach makes sense for what you need to get done. A high return on involvement means you'll see a big payoff in quality, commitment, and productivity from engaging others. A lower return on involvement means you may do the work better alone or with only a few others.

You can see the Return on Involvement Assessment Tool in Figure 1.1.

FIGURE 1.1

THE RETURN ON INVOLVEMENT ASSESSMENT TOOL

Your Own Capability

- Could you complete the work on your own? Would tackling it alone compromise the quality of your work?

How Others Would Feel About Joining You

- Are others likely to see the work as a good investment of their time and energy? Will they be excited to join this effort? Would they feel left out or even resentful if you did not include them?

How Others Could Add Value to Your Efforts

- What benefits could result from involving others in this work?

What It Will Take to Involve Others

- How difficult will it be to get others involved in this work? How much time and energy will be needed to keep them involved?

(*continued*)

Overall Assessment

- How would the benefits from involving others compare to the costs needed to involve them?

- Based on your answers to these questions, does it make sense to involve others?

An engineering manager we know road-tested the Return on Involvement Assessment Tool. He used it in approaching a project to reduce the cycle time it took to make revisions to engineering drawings. Let's follow his line of thinking through his answers to the tool's questions in Figure 1.2.

FIGURE 1.2

THE RETURN ON INVOLVEMENT ASSESSMENT TOOL EXAMPLE

Reducing the Cycle Time to Make Revisions to Engineering Drawings

Your Own Capability

- Could you complete the work on your own? Would tackling it alone compromise the quality of your work?
  - *Engineering Manager Response: I could complete this project on my own with confidence because I have intimate knowledge of where breakdowns occur and how to fix them.*

(continued)

How Others Would Feel About Joining You

- Are others likely to see the work as a good investment of their time and energy? Will they be excited to join this effort? Would they feel left out or even resentful if you did not include them?
  - *Engineering Manager Response: This is a high priority project for the entire engineering organization and for our internal customers, the production organization. A lot of people have a big stake in getting these revisions done faster and would like to help make it happen.*

How Others Could Add Value to Your Efforts

- What benefits could result from involving others in this work?
  - *Engineering Manager Response: I could get this project done on my own, but it would be better to involve others. Together we would probably find more ways to get these revisions done faster. From past experience, I'm sure it will be easier to get these changes implemented if I let more people get involved.*

What It Will Take to Involve Others

- How difficult will it be to get others involved in this work? How much time and energy will be needed to keep them involved?
  - *Engineering Manager Response: Since this is such a critical project, I don't think I will have much trouble getting other people signed up to work on it. I think if we thought it through on the front end, we could develop a plan that would make it pretty easy to keep them involved to see the job through.*

Overall Assessment

- How would the benefits from involving others compare to the costs needed to involve them?
  - *Engineering Manager Response: By involving people from the very beginning, I won't have to spend time convincing them of solutions that I developed. I will also have the benefit of their ideas and as a result the solution will be better.*
- Based on your answers to these questions, does it make sense to involve others?
  - *Engineering Manager Response: Absolutely.*

Now it's your turn. Think of some project or initiative where you might be wondering about whether it makes sense to involve others. Then use the Return on Involvement Assessment Tool to get clearer about whether you should involve others or not.

What Kind of Involvement Do You Need?

If you have decided it makes sense to involve others, you now need to determine the kind of involvement that will be best for your particular situation.

Whether you're acting as a manager at work or welcoming a new puppy into your home, it's important not to be tempted to skip this question. Early on you may feel pulled toward immediate action. Maybe you've got a big assignment that's due soon. Pausing to get clear before you start working may seem like a waste of valuable time. Or maybe you're thinking that this question is overkill for you: "What we're doing is simple. Heck, we could be done in the time it'll take to determine the kind of involvement I need."

These are common feelings. But if you're serious about being an effective involver, it's important to rethink these assumptions. Rather than plunging headfirst into your work, take a "Go slow to go fast" approach. When you invest the time to get clear about the kind of involvement you need, you make it easier for people to join you. You'll be able to easily explain the type of help you need and why you need them to pitch in. People are drawn to clarity. Answer this question well and people will want to work with you.

It may be easiest for you to do this up-front thinking alone, or you may want to ask for help from a few others. Either way, your most important objective is to be able to explain clearly and succinctly the kind of involvement you need and why you've decided on this type.

Consider who, if anyone, can help you get clear. If you want to assemble a core group and haven't yet, do so now. There's no rule about how many people is the right number. Invite enough people to ensure that your initial thinking is solid, but not so many that you get bogged down before you even get started. Don't choose folks with whom you tend to always agree. Reach out to a critical friend. If you pay attention to the big picture, recruit someone who focuses on details. If you're the logical type, find someone who picks up on other people's emotions.

Why Determines How

When you get clear on the reasons you need to involve others in your work, you'll become clear on the kind of involvement you'll need to get the job done.

Here are four basic reasons for reaching out to engage others:

- You need others' specific expertise or "Know-How Involvement"—there are skills and knowledge required that you don't have.
- You need others' help with basic to do's or "Arms and Legs Involvement"—the job is too big for you to get done on your own.
- You need others' buy-in or "Care and Commitment Involvement"—without their long-term commitment you'll never be successful.
- You need others to become more capable in the future or "Teaching and Learning Involvement"—this enables others to take on more responsibilities and frees you to make other contributions.

These different kinds of involvement are not mutually exclusive. In most cases, you'll need to tap into more than one type of involvement to be successful. Let's take a look at the story of Jake and his new puppy that opened this chapter.

Jake needed the Know-How Involvement of the obedience class instructor to tame Theo's rambunctious behavior. He needed the Arms and Legs Involvement of his kids to pitch in with Theo's training when he was out of town. His wife's Care and Commitment Involvement was a critical success factor, because if she didn't buy in to the whole idea of another dog, Theo would never have made it in the front door. And during those hours spent in the yard calling out "Heel, Theo, heel!" Jake needed Teaching and Learning Involvement from the pup so that he didn't face the prospect of losing his voice every time he walked the dog.

Our engineer focused on a different combination of types of involvement in reducing the cycle time it took to make revisions to engineering drawings. He believed he had the knowledge and experience to complete the redesign work on his own, but doing so could have left others confused about why he was making certain changes. They could have objected to his plans. This told him he needed to reach out and create some Care and Commitment Involvement.

By completing his return on involvement analysis, he realized that without involving others, he could also be missing an opportunity to come up with the best solution to his problem. Though he thought he knew enough to solve the problem on his own, it was clear to him that others had experiences and perspectives he did not. So there was also a component of Know-How Involvement he needed to consider as he went about his work.

Let's take a closer look at each of these four kinds of involvement and how you'll know which is your best bet in different situations.

Know-How Involvement.   You use Know-How Involvement to tap into skills, knowledge, or experience that is needed to move your work forward but that you don't possess. Telltale signs that this is the kind of involvement you need include situations where you:

- Realize you lack formal schooling for the work at hand. This is the case, for example, when you could benefit from having a finance expert on a project team at work, a marketing expert for a new program at your local school, or an engineer to help assess the renovations needed at your church.
- Are clear about your current circumstances and where you want to be in the future, but don't see a roadmap for getting from "here" to "there." Architects, interior designers, and general contractors can all help you bring the image of your dream home into focus and lay out the steps to follow in building it. A manager may know specifications for features and pricing of a new product, but she needs members of her development team to chart a course that creates the actual product.
- Might have *some* expertise in a particular area, but where others have more and could do the job better, faster, or cheaper. Yes, you might eventually get that new disposal installed in the kitchen, but a professional plumber could have it done this afternoon, putting you in a much better mood for going out on the town later that night. At work, you might have come up through the ranks as an engineer and still be less than an expert when it comes to the latest software. This is a time to make use of Know-How Involvement.

Arms and Legs Involvement.   You use Arms and Legs Involvement to check off to do's when the list is too long for you to tackle on your own. You've got the know-how, but the scope of work exceeds your time and energy or you'd be better off applying your expertise in other ways. Here are some situations that set off warning bells that it's time to reach out for this kind of involvement:

- The work is simple and repetitive—easily done by another. When it's time to move to a new home, close friends sometimes pitch in to help you pack. You might even hire parts of the job out to professional movers. Retail businesses are famous for an "all hands on deck" approach to sales days when people come flocking in and the standard shift assignments alone would lead to long lines and disgruntled customers.
- The amount of work is more than you can handle on your own. Have you ever signed on to organize the Christmas tree sales or car washing fundraisers for your child's scout or youth group? Imagine the hours you'd have spent freezing or soaked if other parents had not contributed their fair share. If you've ever had a hand in setting up for a large meeting or trade show at work, you know firsthand the benefits of Arms and Legs Involvement.
- Your time could be better spent doing other things. Hiring out your lawn care, house cleaning, or even the babysitter on Saturday night are all examples of this kind of involvement. Public transportation such as buses and trains are another example of this type of involvement. They make it possible to finish a final edit on a paper or catch a catnap on the way to and from work.

Care and Commitment Involvement. You use Care and Commitment Involvement to create buy-in from others to the work you need to do. This type of involvement is called for when:

- The work you are doing involves change. Without others' caring and commitment, you'll never implement your best-laid plans. At a personal level, marriage is a great example requiring this kind of involvement. It can represent the single greatest change in your life. Without deep caring and commitment, couples never stand a chance of adapting to the many changes that go hand-in-hand with those vows. When you think about getting people on board with new strategies or ways of working in organizations, Caring and Commitment Involvement is what you're after.
- You need people to stay involved over an extended period of time. If you agree to take tickets at the door for your church's annual fundraiser, that's Arms and Legs Involvement. But if you've chaired the planning subcommittee for the six months leading up to the gala event, you're clearly in Care and Commitment Involvement territory. The best teams you've been part of have featured this type of involvement. You were in it together over the long haul to accomplish shared goals.

- The work before you will be difficult or you're not certain of success. This is when people's extra effort can make the difference between success and failure. Families need this level of extraordinary involvement when a child is failing school or an elderly parent needs to move in with adult children. In both cases, the path ahead will be challenging and you'll have an easier time navigating these uncharted waters with a healthy dose of Care and Commitment Involvement. Turning around a company that's in danger of going out of business or being acquired is an example of the same dynamic in a business setting.

Teaching and Learning Involvement.   You use Teaching and Learning Involvement to build others' skills and knowledge so they become more capable of doing their work in the future. Situations where this type of involvement is needed include:

- When others want to grow and develop and seek you out as a mentor (or vice versa). This is one of the highest compliments you can be paid—others value what you're doing and how you're doing it so much that they're asking you to be their personal coach. An informal cup of coffee once a month with the immediate past president of the community board you're now heading up is an example of this. You may have hit it off with a boss early in your career whom you still stay in touch with and whose advice you value.
- When an organization makes a conscious effort to develop people in it. This is where formal programs come into play. Your church, temple, or mosque likely has scripture classes or study groups available so congregation members can learn more about their religion and live in line with its teachings. You may also have a development plan with a career ladder at your workplace. The company's course offerings are all part of a planned effort for you to develop and become a more valuable contributor.
- When you know there is other important work for you to do, if only there were someone who could do what you're now doing. It's a great gift when you're headed out of town for a well-deserved vacation if your kids know how to cook dinner for themselves.

Think of the time that you'll have available for packing before you leave instead of slaving away in the kitchen preparing a week's worth of dinners. When some in your company learn how to take the lead in keeping the daily operations humming, it creates valuable time for you and others to begin planning for the future.

Getting clear on the kind of involvement you need by using the tools we've provided will generate your excitement and energy around the work ahead. Furthermore, it's a different kind of energy than if you'd started with an immediate rush into activity. Rather than feeling under the gun—"The clock is ticking!"—you'll feel grounded and quietly confident about your ability to engage others. You can never guarantee smooth sailing for all your work. But rough seas can be minimized if you get clear on the kind of involvement you need before you get started.

Different Kinds of Involvement: A Case Study

It's important to always stay clear about what you are trying to accomplish since different goals call for different kinds of involvement. Here's a story that illustrates the point.

A Jewish temple and an Episcopal church share a building in Ann Arbor, Michigan—the longest-standing affiliation of its type in America. Some years ago, the temple and church were in conflict, which threatened the harmony of the relationship. The membership of the temple was growing, but that of the church was not. Members of the temple wanted a larger social hall for celebrating life-cycle events in their community—weddings, bar and bat mitzvahs, and so on. The church wanted to invest its excess funds in charitable works. Initially the boards of each organization met together to see if they could iron out their differences.

After these sessions, the temple leaders thought that the project was clear: the work they faced was to decide whether or not to build an expanded social hall. They planned to hold a few meetings with the board's audit committee to determine the financial feasibility of such an effort (Know-How Involvement). They talked about what it would take to encourage members of the congregation to contribute to a fundraising campaign (a creative variation of Arms and Legs Involvement you might call "Checkbook and Wallet Involvement"). But as they explored the situation further, they uncovered a more fundamental question: "What kind of temple do we want to be?"

Suddenly, the entire project changed. The temple leadership knew they needed to engage the entire congregation in such a significant question. Through a series of congregation-wide meetings, temple members joined together in conversations about their collective future (Care and Commitment Involvement). A vision for the temple community gradually emerged. At the same time, they also got clearer about the nature of their relationship with their church partners. This new clarity made it relatively easy to resolve the building issues. They proceeded to build a beautiful new worship area, social hall, and educational classrooms that have benefited both congregations—with strong backing from across the congregations' members.

Today, the space shared by the temple and the church is the best-utilized building in Ann Arbor. Schools, community groups, fitness classes, and lifetime learning programs are all housed there for below-market fees. This met the church's need for charitable works. These various groups have also provided a substantial source of income, defraying the costs borne by the temple and church for the construction project. The lesson: as you get clearer about what you're trying to accomplish, you'll get clearer about the kinds of involvement you need.

Chapter Checklist

The sequence for getting clear on the kind of involvement you need is:

- Use the Return on Involvement Assessment Tool to think through the risks and rewards of involving others in your work or going it alone.
- Based on this analysis, determine if it makes sense to tackle the work in front of you without involving anyone else. If it does, go to it and get the job done.
- If you've gotten clear that you want to include others in your efforts, decide what kind of involvement will be most useful in your particular circumstances:
  - Know-How Involvement
  - Arms and Legs Involvement
  - Caring and Commitment Involvement
  - Teaching and Learning Involvement

Chapter 2

HOW DO I KNOW WHOM TO INCLUDE?

A wedding is a good example of the challenges and complexities of involvement. It's certainly something that is hard to do alone. And anyone who has ever planned a wedding knows that the question, "Whom will we include?" is a big, big deal.

The kind of wedding we want has a big influence on whom we invite. The answer can range from the Las Vegas quickie to a wedding on a royal scale at St. Paul's Cathedral. If the couple chooses the Las Vegas option, fewer people are involved than in the royal scale wedding, which involves many people and many decisions. Most people come out somewhere in between.

Usually, the bride makes a list and the groom makes a list. Their lists include people they *want* to have there (like their best friends from school and their favorite aunts and uncles) as well as people they feel obligated to ask (like grouchy cousin Lula and brother-in-law Jack, who always gets drunk at weddings). Clashes arise between bride and groom over the size of their lists and specific inclusions and exclusions (such as old flames and buddies considered obnoxious by the opposite party). Eventually the parents of the bride and groom (who are often helping to pay for the whole deal) weigh in with their lists, including local friends and neighbors, business associates, and distant relatives who have never even met the bride and groom. The numbers begin to expand.

Soon the thinking turns to the support needed for the kind of wedding wanted: whom to include in the wedding party, the kind of clothing, the time of the event, the photographer, the videographer, the menu, the music, who sits with whom, and whose family tradition we follow for the first dance. Soon the mushrooming numbers rub up against such practical realities as the size of the catering hall and the budget. Sometimes the conflicts become so intense that the young lovers decide to elope instead—or call off the wedding altogether.

The kind of wedding we choose will determine whom to include and when. It raises issues dealing with different points of view, influence, and budget while at the same time keeping the fundamental goal in mind: making this a memorable and meaningful event for those getting married.

Just as people planning weddings often worry about whom to include, people in organizations worry about whom to include to get things done. Whether you are planning a wedding or your next staff meeting or leading a work initiative, whom to include is a big deal.

In answering the question, "How do I know whom to include?" we focus on three points:

- How do I involve more than the usual people?
- How many people should I include?
- Should the same people be involved throughout all the work?

How Do I Involve More Than the Usual People?

In Chapter 1, you learned the importance of being clear about what you want to accomplish and what kind of involvement is needed. This determines the kind of people you need to include.

You probably have some people in mind to include in the work already. Some people are obvious choices because they match the work to be done due to the passion they exhibit, the knowledge and experience they bring, or the personal and political clout they wield.

But beyond these obvious choices, it's helpful to have a framework for thinking about whom to include, one that will challenge you to think outside the box about those you might want to invite. Think beyond the people whom you normally invite, the "people who do everything" in your organization or community. (You know who they are—the usual suspects.) Make a deliberate effort to include people who may stretch, challenge, or change your usual way of thinking.

A police department in England was working on the design of a new jail cell. In an effort to stretch their thinking, the design committee decided to include members of a group most often ignored, though most directly affected—the prisoners themselves. The prisoners came up with a number of important contributions. For example, they pointed out that installing the cell door so that the hinge faced outward would reduce suicides by eliminating one surface on which a rope or bed sheet could be hung. This life-saving insight could only be offered by someone who had spent long hours of loneliness and despair staring at a cell door—a vivid example of the value of including in your work participants who are normally excluded.

For all but the simplest work, get the advice of others before you shape your final invitation list. Simply asking the question, "Who else needs to be here?" will open up possibilities you otherwise would have missed. This model's broad involvement, at a very early stage in the development of your work, sets a tone that will be increasingly valuable as the work proceeds. Remember John Donne's observation: "No man is an island, entire of itself."

If you are considering whom to invite to the next staff meeting, ask those present at the current meeting, "Who needs to be here?" If you are considering a larger initiative, then you need to convene a group to help plan whom to involve that mirrors those involved and impacted.

Here is a framework to help you involve more than the usual people. It identifies six important categories to consider, each of which brings something different to the work. They are:

- People who care
- People with authority and responsibility
- People with information and expertise
- People who will be personally affected
- People with diverse points of view
- People who are considered troublemakers

Let's talk about these categories in more detail.

People Who Care.   People who care have passion, consider the work important, and are ready to devote their energy to ensuring a good outcome. They come in many types, including people who have a stake in the outcome of the work and people whose children the work might influence.

One way to find out who cares is to ask for volunteers—people who have a choice about whether to participate, not those who are told that they must come. When we volunteer time and energy, it shows we care.

In Naperville, Illinois, a town of 130,000, the local school district was planning a conference to create a vision for students in the twenty-first century. They decided to include some 300 people in creating the vision. The invitation list included students, teachers, and administrators; parents; representatives of local businesses that had partnered with the school system; and members of the larger community, such as a professor from the education department at a local university, local religious leaders, and city and county officials. They also wanted volunteers from the community, so they created a video for local cable television explaining the work and asking community members to participate in the conference. Articles in local newspapers were also used to invite participants.

Three hundred people became involved, including those who worked for the school system and were invited as well as volunteers from the community. They all gave two and a half days of their time to the effort, demonstrating vividly the depth of their commitment to the Naperville school district and its educational mission.

Some initiatives are more conducive to volunteering than others. If your work includes tasks that can be performed with minimal specific expertise, on an open schedule with flexible guidelines and quality standards, then volunteering can play a significant role. In our experience, there are few projects to which volunteers cannot contribute.

The next question is how many volunteers should be included. We've seen organizations dedicate anywhere from 5 percent to 70 percent of the slots in each group to volunteers. If they get more volunteers than there are slots available, participants are selected randomly—drawing names from a hat, for instance—and in public, so that the process remains transparent.

People with Authority and Responsibility.   People with authority and responsibility are important to the success of the work. We need them because they have unique information to share and control over necessary support and resources. People with authority and responsibility can run interference with the powers that be, win or grant approvals, and champion the work at higher levels of government, business, or civic society. They also follow up on the work and ensure that it is institutionalized or folded into the organization as the organization grows and changes.

In a meeting about restructuring the human resources department of an international airline, two options emerged, each with strong support. After extensive debate, a vote was taken. Option A won by a single vote. It was a moment of truth for the group. Given the narrow margin of victory, would debate resume, or would the organization move forward?

After a moment of silence, the corporation's vice president for human resources spoke up. "Clearly we have a house divided. Both options are attractive. But a decision must be made. In keeping with our democratic tradition, we will abide by the will of the majority. We'll follow Option A."

Of all the people in the room, only the vice president had both the authority and the responsibility to make this decision. (She also had the personal courage to do so.) If she had not been in the room, it's likely that the debate would have continued for the rest of the day. Instead, the group was able to move on and successfully implement Option A.

People with Information and Expertise.   People with information and expertise offer crucial insights from many parts of an organization or community. They represent various hierarchical levels, functions, and periods of organizational memory. They also provide technical expertise that may be needed, such as financial acumen, marketing savvy, or computer skills.

When a major hospital system wanted to create a vision for the future of their organization, the planners understood the importance of including a broad range of information and expertise providers. Their list of invitees included physicians from every hospital department, nurses representing each health care function, support staff (such as secretaries and maintenance workers), administrators and corporate staff members, patients (both satisfied and dissatisfied), insurance company representatives, health care consultants, and members of similar organizations that had conducted similar projects. Only by gathering all these diverse people in one room could the system hope to develop a future vision that was both broad and soundly based in the realities of the changing world of health care.

People Who Will Be Personally Affected.   People who will be personally affected by the work need and deserve a place at the table. They might include workers whose jobs will change, clients whose experience of the organization will be altered, members of other organizations whose contacts will be affected by the project, and community members whose lives will be impacted and changed.

Involving a range of people who will be affected by any change sends an important message of empowerment. At one high-tech manufacturing plant, the supply chain that controlled the flow of raw materials into the factory as well as the development and shipping of finished products out of the factory was badly flawed. Several large meetings were held where customers, suppliers, workers, and managers came together to discuss the problems and create a new design for the supply chain.

In the midst of these conversations, one line worker at the plant who had been having difficulty getting a crucial part from a supplier took it upon himself to call the president of the supplier company. He explained the situation and got the part he needed the next day. Being involved in the supply chain design project had enabled this worker to take ownership of the problem and move forcefully to solve it.

People with Diverse Points of View.   People with different points of view may include people who have minority opinions, people opposed to what is going on, people who play a different role in the organization or community, or people who represent a particular race, gender, age, or other significant characteristic.

You may feel reluctant—perhaps unconsciously—to include people with different points of view. After all, won't dissenting voices just slow us down and prevent progress? Actually, the opposite may be true. Our experience has shown that the more points of view that are heard and understood during the development of any project, the more innovative the solutions devised. Bringing in people with different points of view is the only way to uncover what they all have in common and are willing to work for.

Troublemakers.   The sixth category of people to include is the troublemakers. Who are the troublemakers? In the typical workplace, organization, or community, most people know who the troublemakers are. They are the resistors, the dominators, and the detractors. They are the people who refuse to be team players. They irritate, annoy, alienate, and just plain bother everyone they come into contact with.

Why include troublemakers in your work? One reason is that troublemakers are centers of organizational energy. We prefer having the troublemaker using energy inside the work rather than stirring up trouble and distrust from the outside. If the troublemakers are working with us, we can welcome them, try to see the world through their eyes, treat them with respect, and find what is valuable in their input.

At a company where planning was under way to implement a new program of self-directed teamwork, one union steward was generally considered a troublemaker because she was always filing grievances. After much internal debate, the planning group decided to invite the steward to join. To widespread surprise, she became instrumental in leading the effort. The reason? For the first time, the steward had found a place where her voice would be heard and her concerns would be taken seriously.

In Figure 2.1, we present a simple tool to use in thinking about whom to include in your next work initiative. When first using this tool, fill in the types of people such as customers, suppliers, and partners, then in the next column brainstorm the actual names of people to include.

Some people find a visual map useful in helping them see who should be involved. This is another way to trigger your thinking to be more participative. Remember the school district that was working on a vision for the twenty-first century? After thinking through the categories of people they wanted to include, they created a visual map like the one in Figure 2.2 as a tool for identifying types of people that ought to participate. As the planning meeting began, they wrote the name of the district in the middle of the map, then invited people to call out the kinds of people that they saw as key to this event. The recorder wrote them on the map like branches on a tree. As a result, they saw that several of the categories produced the same kinds of roles and they were able to more easily attach names to the roles.

FIGURE 2.1

THE WHOM TO INVOLVE TOOL

Work Name: _____

Categories	Types	Names
People who care		
People with authority and responsibility		
People with information and expertise		
People who will be personally affected		
People with diverse points of view		
People who are considered troublemakers		

Figure 2.2

THE WHOM TO INVOLVE MAP FOR THE NAPERVILLE, ILLINOIS, SCHOOL DISTRICT 203

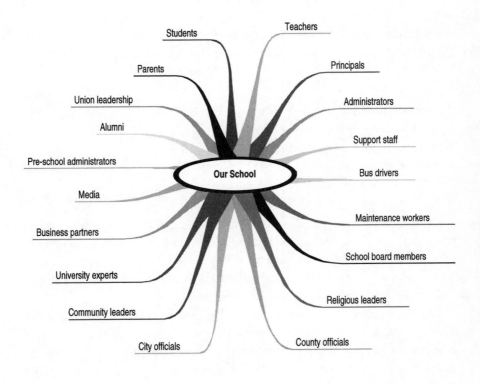

How Many People Should I Include?

How to involve the right number of people is a concern shared by many involvers. If you involve too many people, you might not get the work done effectively because there are too many opinions to consider. If you involve too few, you might not get new thinking. You might also miss people who will help implement and coordinate the work.

Don't assume that limiting the number of people involved will save you time and money. This assumption overlooks the costs associated with neglected points of view, limited perspectives, and the resistance that occurs when important people are left out of the conversation. And don't assume that involving lots of people guarantees you success.

A printing plant was transforming itself to a team-based organization. Although they involved customers and suppliers in their redesign, they neglected to involve the company's sales force. Why was this important? Because the sales force determined where products would be printed. As the plant's culture began to shift, the sales force became nervous because things were done differently in the team-based plant. Consequently, the sales force was reluctant to assign product to this plant. Excluding the sales force's voice in the transformation had unintended negative consequences for the plant.

As a general rule, the number of people to include depends on five key questions:

- How much energy do you want to create?
- How large is the scope of the task?
- How much time is available?
- How many people are needed to keep other organizational functions running?
- How much money can you spend?

If you want to create a lot of energy, larger groups are the most effective. These are best for system analysis and visioning. Smaller groups are best for doing detail work and working on smaller jobs. Furthermore, a large group is useful when you want to create a critical mass for change within the broader organization or community.

Consider, too, that the number of people you involve is likely to change over time. If the scope of the work is big, you will involve larger numbers of people. If it is narrower, then fewer people can do it. Many initiatives involve both large and small groups at various points in the life of the work.

The Naperville School District that was working on a vision for education in the twenty-first century had several groups of different sizes:

- A small combined group of four from the school board and administration determined the kind of visioning process they wished to engage in. They then organized a planning group of around twenty people to represent all constituencies. This group formed committees to work on logistics, communication, and invitations.
- A large group of 300 came together to create the vision.
- Ten task forces of approximately eight to fifteen people were formed by volunteers around the themes of the vision to recommend ways to implement them. The task forces added new members who were interested and had a member of the planning team to coordinate with the larger group.

Involving people is not always such a complex undertaking. For example, moving a piano requires a small group of people to move the piano from here to there. You need a few strong bodies and at least one person who can think visually so the piano doesn't get stuck when you're trying to round the corner going up the stairs.

In working with clients, we use a concept called "critical mass" to identify the people that you must involve in order to succeed. Critical mass means enough of the right people to accomplish what you need to in any particular effort. What is your critical mass for this work? From the original list of brainstormed invitees, who *must* be involved? These are the people who could make or break your effort.

Then move to the next layer of people. Who would be nice to keep involved? These people would make everyone's job easier, but if push came to shove, you could get by without them. Finally, is there anyone who would be okay not to involve? What are the consequences if they are not involved?

It may be helpful to fill in the worksheet in Figure 2.3 to get clear on these questions.

FIGURE 2.3

THE CRITICAL MASS WORKSHEET TOOL

People we *must* have involved   Why?

People we'd *like* to have involved   Why?

People that would be okay *not* to involve   Why?

Using this tool helps you determine the number of people that you need to involve and why you need to involve them. This can also help you be respectful of their time if you are clear about how you wish to involve them.

Should the Same People Be Involved Throughout All the Work?

Sometimes everyone included is on board throughout. Sometimes some of the players change, as different knowledge, viewpoints, and skills are needed, while a core of people remains to provide continuity. In small jobs such as planning an awards banquet for the soccer team, you want the same crew involved throughout. In larger initiatives such as the Naperville Futures Project, some people change as the work changes.

Involving the right folks at the right time in the life of an initiative is crucial to its success. It infuses energy, stimulates creative solutions, and ensures that the right decisions are made. It also produces a set of champions who will act as advocates, marketers, and salespeople in the broader organization or community, ultimately involving many more people in the final implementation of your work.

By contrast, when the wrong people are involved, progress is likely to be slow. Because the necessary talents and knowledge are missing from around the table, flawed decisions are made and creative energy becomes dissipated. If you complete your planning efforts, support from the broader community may be lacking because key influencers are uninvolved or even actively hostile.

As you think about whom to involve at what stage of the job, keep in mind the following suggestions:

- In the early stages, you want people who are visionary and creative.
- When you want to review work done so far, you want people who are challenging, reflective, and honest.
- When you need to reach consensus, you want people who are collaborative, realistic, and unselfish.
- When you are doing detail work, you want people who are concrete, thorough, and meticulous.

Figure 2.4 presents a tool to use to prompt your thinking.

FIGURE 2.4

THE TYPES OF PEOPLE TO INCLUDE AT DIFFERENT STAGES TOOL

Stage	Tasks	Types of People	Names
Early			
• Decide on the work and what kind of involvement is ineeded • Whom to include • How to invite them	• Gather information • Identify possibilities • Sort options • Discuss pros and cons • Decide	• Knowledgeable • Open minded • Visionary • Creative	
Middle			
• How to keep people involved	• Keep purpose front and center • Let people know how we are doing • Support people who are involved • Regularly reassess the kind of involvement needed • Stay open to those with differing points of view • Appreciate what people can contribute	• Challenging • Reflective • Collaborative • Meticulous • Honest	
Late			
• How to finish the job	• Bring things to a close • Identify key events • Discuss experiences • Capture lessons	• Thorough • Concrete • Reflective • Curious • Honest	

Chapter Checklist

The sequence for deciding whom to include in your work is:

- Think about how to involve more than the usual people based on the six categories: people who care, people with authority and responsibility, people with information and expertise, people who will be personally affected, people with diverse points of view, and people who are considered troublemakers.
- When considering how many people to include, think whom you must have to succeed and who would be nice to have to support the work.
- When thinking about whom to involve at what stage, chunk out what you see as the stages and think through the characteristics of people you would like to include. Remember you'll have to adjust as you go along due to unplanned circumstances.

Chapter 3

HOW DO I INVITE PEOPLE TO BECOME INVOLVED?

Julie once received an invitation to a garden party at Buckingham Palace hosted by the Queen of England. Yes, *that* Queen of England. Julie had to sign a receipt when the invitation was delivered. The envelope was stamped front and back with "Lord Chamberlain Buckingham Palace." It was addressed in beautifully handwritten calligraphic script. The message on the card itself was embossed in gold. It began with the words "The Lord Chamberlain is commanded to invite . . . "

Talk about a special invitation. Julie still has it. The Queen, and the Lord Chamberlain, could be sure she would be there.

If we are not going to do it alone then we have to do something to invite others to join us. We know the people we want. Getting them to come becomes our focus.

We may not be confident they will come. We might fear that they won't find what we are inviting them to exciting or worthwhile. Then they might think less of us. We could worry that it will take a lot of work to persuade them. It's the times when we are not sure how to invite people in, when we are not confident that they will come, that this step deals with.

In answering the question, "How do I invite people to become involved?" we focus on six things:

- The list of people we want to invite
- How to invite them
- Making it personal
- Asking them to do something
- Dealing with objections
- Following up

Now you may be thinking that inviting people just takes some common sense. We might find it very simple: Give them a call, or have a chat as we pass them on the street or in the corridor, and they readily join us. Why go through all this to invite someone to join us?

But our experience is that when the stakes are high, "common sense" goes out the window. When time is tight and we are under pressure, we use the methods that are easiest for us rather than the ones most likely to tempt people to join us. How often do you send a quick e-mail to twenty people announcing a meeting and then find that only three or four people took enough notice of it to show up?

We can easily make assumptions about what people need. This might mean that we give them too much information, which ends up being off-putting, and they turn us down because they think they will not be able to cope. On the other hand, we can send something out in a rush and give too little information. Then they don't join us because they did not have enough information to know they would want to.

Our six focus areas can serve as gentle reminders to guide us in these situations.

The List of People We Want to Invite

If your involvement work is on track, Chapter 2 will have challenged you to consider inviting extraordinary people into your work. You should now be looking at a list of names. The list will include people who care, people with authority and responsibility, people with information and expertise, people who will be personally affected, people with diverse points of view, and people who are considered troublemakers. You might not have lists of names for each of the categories of people, but you will have an idea about how you might reach them.

You should also have decided how many people you want to involve in the work. You should have gone through the ideas generated by the categories and considered who was essential and who was desirable. If your work is complex, you may even have completed separate lists of people for each phase of the work.

We deliberately take the question of whom to invite and separate it from the question of how to invite them. Then any nervousness about actually issuing an invitation won't deter us from putting people on the list.

We have heard people use "They won't come" as a reason to eliminate people from involvement. Guess what? If you don't even ask them, they won't.

In Julie's house, they called this kind of speaking for other people "tractoring." The word comes from a story Julie's dad used to tell about a farmer whose tractor breaks down. He decides to ask a neighbor if he can borrow his tractor. On the way to the neighboring farm, the farmer thinks about the man he is going to see. He remembers stories he heard about other people being refused favors, and he remembers something he borrowed from this farmer a while ago and has not yet returned. He begins to wonder whether the farmer will lend him the tractor and becomes more and more anxious about asking. Finally, when he gets to the door and rings the bell, the neighbor cheerfully answers, and the farmer angrily says, "You can keep your bleeping tractor!"

Don't tractor—don't speak for other people.

How challenging is your list? Do you wonder if some of the people you've listed will come? Are you beginning to think about not even asking them? Does the thought of asking them make you nervous? Nervous is good. You can tap into your nervousness and use it to inspire you to invite with confidence and originality.

How you invite people can be critical to your success in involving them and getting things done. It is worth being creative about finding ways to invite the people on your list to join you that are compelling and galvanizing. Here are a few ways to be compelling:

- Sometimes just telling people about the activity you want to involve them in is compelling. We barely need asking twice to a close friend's birthday or wedding celebration.
- On the phone, in the corridors, and in presentations, talk about your project in a way that is galvanizing. When you speak with passion, people will want to join you.
- The form of the invitation can be unusual. We once saw people being invited to a farmer's market with apple-shaped balloons.
- Sometimes the name or the title of the work can be intriguing. One pharmaceutical company who wanted to invite people to join them in developing a new identity for their website called it "The Mad Hatter's Tea Party" and invited people to "come and lose their marbles" with an activity using marbles.

Or you can have another type of creative theme. We have seen many other themes with invitations to match, from "movie tickets" for a research project in Cannes during the Film Festival, to "travel passes" to invite people to join a Learning Journey project, to footballs to tempt people to join in work on values at a football field.

When you focus on the list of people you want to involve, use it to inspire and motivate you. You are not going to be doing this alone. All these people may join you. You are going to get great things done.

How to Invite Them

There are a lot of ways to invite people. Sit now and think of all the things you have been invited to join. You did not say yes to them all. Which stood out for you as ones you knew instantly you were attracted to? Was it just the appeal of the job? Was there something about the way you were asked that made it appealing? Or was it the person who asked?

Let's consider many of the options. If time permits, we might put out feelers during a casual lunchtime conversation. If time is tight, we might send an e-mail. We could craft a letter, a card, a leaflet, or some other kind of written invitation. We can use a phone call or a personal visit. We can invite people during meetings and presentations. Each form of invitation has its strengths and weaknesses.

Face-to-Face. This is the most powerful medium for persuasion. You are showing that you have clearly made an investment to spend time with the people you are inviting. You will be able to see how people are responding, which can help you tailor your message appropriately. You can deal with objections straight away.

We worked on a project in Liverpool where the planning team made the effort to go out personally to many community groups and invite them directly. Needless to say, going to see people face-to-face takes a lot of time. Even if you go around and see them in groups, it could take a while to get things moving.

Another version of face-to-face is the video conference call. This cuts out the travel of a personal meeting. It might not be ideal for a first invitation, but may be used to issue a broader invitation once a project has started.

Phone. The personal nature of a phone invitation can be persuasive. The phone allows for a conversation, which also gives us the opportunity to answer questions. We might think it more difficult to use the phone for large projects with a number of people making the calls. We have seen teams plan a phone message carefully so that they can all be as compelling. This was not in the form of a rigid script but simply a basic format of points to mention. In a business context, we've found it can be very powerful when a senior manager makes the call. If your company CEO phoned to invite you to join a project, wouldn't you be eager to agree?

Of course, the biggest problem with the phone is calling the people you don't know. Just the thought of it can make us go cold. The trick is to think of it like a meeting. In Chapter 6, we introduce a framework for meetings that you can use when making cold calls. Once you have introduced yourself, form some kind of connection. You could mention the person who suggested you call them. Talk with them about the issues in the work, listen, and note their ideas. Invite them to begin to share ideas about what is possible and plan with them some things that you could do. As you do this, you will draw them in and asking them will be easy.

Letters, Cards, and Leaflets.   Printed documents are a good choice when your invitation list includes a number of people you do not know. They offer a lot of scope for creativity. We've seen stunning leaflets that use unusual typestyles, shapes, colors, graphics, and paper choices to create a powerful impact. You can use themes and wacky titles. A well-crafted personal letter can also be extremely effective.

The trouble with these kinds of written invites is that they can seem very formal. They also have to compete with all the other things people get in the mail.

E-mail.   This is an increasingly common method of issuing invitations, although it has serious drawbacks. Most people today have electronic in-boxes filled with messages, and separating the important messages from the spam is a time-consuming and annoying chore. Still, e-mail offers unsurpassed speed and efficiency.

When you know your audience well, and especially when they are expecting a message from you (and therefore are unlikely to overlook it), e-mail can be effective.

You might want to consider ways to make your e-mail work better as a way of inviting people. We like to see color and web links. We are drawn to simple short messages and the sense that people have taken the time to think about us in writing the e-mail (not just lumped us in with a general distribution). These days using jazzy titles for e-mail can be risky; we have deleted at least one invitation thinking it was spam.

Posters and Advertisements.   When the list of people includes people you are not sure how to reach, consider using well-placed posters to catch people's attention. If you can, tap the talents of an experienced artist or designer to create your posters; they need to be bright, easy to read, and eye-catching. You can also use the press as a conduit for your message; for example, we have been successful in recruiting people to public conferences using a combination of press releases and advertisements.

The serious downside of posters and ads is that some people (including the people you want to reach) may not see them. Worse still, the people you had rather not see them do! Posters and ads can be undiscriminating. You have to be sure you want all comers.

When you are focusing on using the right media, be prepared to consider all options. If necessary, use a combination of two or three media.

Making It Personal

We may not be inviting people to Buckingham Palace, but we can still make people feel special when we invite them to join us. There are many ways to accomplish this. The key, for us, is speaking personally to the people you are inviting and conveying the message "Come in—this will be worth your time."

This is as important in a corporate setting as it is anywhere else. It is easy for people to feel lost in the body corporate and to think that their voice does not matter. In a corporate setting, your request will be competing with many demands. It will sit alongside all the other meetings, e-mail, letters, notices, and phone calls. Making it personal can help it stand out.

Showing that you have thought about the person you are inviting and his or her particular talents, concerns, and aspirations can be powerful. When you help people see what they bring to the party and how their peculiar talents and backgrounds relate directly to your work, they are more likely to join in. Try this: Go through the list of people you created in Chapter 2. Take stock of what you know about them. How busy are they? Have they signed up for work with you in the past? Are they likely to volunteer easily, or will they need persuasion? What are they interested in? What might they be concerned about? What do they care a lot about?

If you know little or nothing about some of the people you are inviting, do a little background research. Talk to them directly, or talk with other people who know them and have involved them in projects in the past. Find out what might encourage them to volunteer. Work hard to build up a clear picture of what might appeal to them. Express your openness to having people offer gifts that are unexpected.

It can be helpful to think of inviting people to join you as a strategic activity. You may find you need different strategies for different people, such as:

- Different ways to make it personal—what will be a hook for one person might not work for another.
- Diverse descriptions of what the work is to match varied talents.
- A range of media—some will read and respond to e-mail, others will need that call.
- A set of tactics for following up.

You can use the Invitation Strategizing Tool (Figure 3.1) as a handy guide to the various tasks involved in answering the question, "How do I invite people to become involved?" Adapt the form in Figure 3.1, adding as many spaces as you need to cover all the people you will be inviting.

Another way we make it personal is by speaking from the heart. As you prepare to invite each person to join you, get in touch with your emotions. Share your deepest desires, dreams, and concerns. Tell people why this venture is important to you and about the important difference you hope to make in the life of your organization or community.

You also make it personal when you make people feel special. When we are inviting people to join us, we can do a lot to make people feel needed and important. Just the request can be enough. If the people you invite can see your passion and imagination, they will be more willing to offer theirs. Don't be afraid to be vulnerable. Be ready to say, "We can't do this without you." The more energy you devote to the process of inviting people, the more likely you are to get an active response.

Figure 3.1

The Invitation Strategizing Tool

People	Relevant Personal Information	Points to Make	Media	Responses and Follow-up

FIGURE 3.2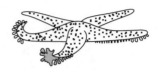

AN IMAGINATIVE INVITATION

A man was walking on the beach and saw a small boy throwing starfish into the ocean. There were millions of them washed up on the shore. "What difference, young man," he asked, "can that possibly make, throwing starfish one at a time?" The boy just picked up another starfish, tossed it into the sea and said: "It'll make a big difference to this one."

Dear

I am writing to you because I think you might be a starfish-thrower. I think you may be someone who, even when faced with a large, seemingly impossible task, will give your all to do whatever you can to make things better. I think you are probably the sort of person who feels that way about our town. If you are such a person I would like to draw on your enthusiasm, love of our town, commitment to make things better, as well as insights, and involve you in the planning of an event that I believe could benefit our town greatly. . . .

Figure 3.2 shows an example of a very distinctive invitation sent by the Reverend David Beedon to key people in the town of Wednesbury, UK.

Finally, including a surprise and making it distinctive will demonstrate that you care. When you do something unusual in your invitations, you lift people out of the everyday. People will be intrigued and wonder what it might be like to be involved in your project. The Body Shop International once sent out invitations to attend an International Franchise Meeting that included an audiotape featuring provocative interviews about change. This unusual step prepared people for a very different gathering.

Asking Them to Do Something

When we invite people to help us get things done, we never intend to waste their time. But they may not believe that. Past experience in being asked to help and then being left on the sidelines, ignored, or other such horror stories of involvement may have colored their view. We can help overcome this by being clear in the invitation what we are asking people to do and why.

Let people know what your project will be like through your invitation. If the work will be creative, then show creativity in the way you invite them. If you will be asking a lot of questions, include several examples in your invitation so that people will start thinking about them and will want to be part of creating the answers.

Sometimes saying what the project will *not* be like is important. We have seen invitations that promise "No speeches, no hierarchy." Those weary of bureaucratic committee meetings are likely to find such an invitation very appealing.

One restructuring project we worked on with a cosmetics company needed people to join at every stage of the design. They wanted everyone to be involved in some part of the job. They laid out what all the work was. They made it clear that each stage of the work required people to do something. They laid out what talents and aptitudes would suit which work. Then they invited people to choose. Everyone responded to this invitation; every stage had a great team of people who came with their sleeves rolled up.

Sometimes we are asking people for their ideas. We might issue a general invitation and get nothing. Ever opened a suggestion box to find that the only slips in the box are sarcastic comments? Perhaps we need to do more than ask them to do something. We might have to say what the impact of their action will be and how we will use it. The best suggestion schemes we have seen have made promises. There was a process that took every suggestion seriously and responded to each one.

Inviting people to meetings can be the hardest work of all. In Chapter 6, we will talk about how you can make meetings a powerhouse of involvement. But you have to get people to show up first. There have been too many meetings that were a waste of their time. If they are wary of meetings, you may need to tell them what work will be done at the meeting. In addition, asking them what they would like to discuss or what should be on the agenda is a powerful way to invite people to your meeting. In doing so, you convey the message "This is not just *my* meeting, it is *our* meeting."

We have seen a range of ways of inviting people to meetings and letting them know that something will be done. One we like is to include some form of interview or questionnaire. It says we are going to be listening to you; you are going to have a say in how this works. Another is to engage people emotionally by asking them to bring something with them—an object or newspaper article—that represents an important issue you are going to be working on in the meeting.

Sometimes you can invite people in by simply getting on with the work yourself. We think of this as "being the invitation." It's one thing to ask people to help you with a job. It's quite another to roll up your sleeves and start doing it yourself. This can work wonders when you are confident that people will recognize that the job is too big for you to handle alone. Also, they can see exactly what you need help with. We have spouses who are masters of this—when they start a big project like redecorating the house or landscaping the garden, it's almost impossible to resist getting involved.

Dealing with Objections

It is natural for people to raise objections. Some will readily join you. Others may have a range of reasons not to.

It can help to have in mind the types of objections people will raise when you invite them and how you are going to respond to them prior to inviting them. Our main thinking about how to deal with the objections is to put yourself in their shoes and think about why they might be raising those objections. Then respond in ways that deal with their objections as you continue to invite them in.

"I'm not sure I have the time to do this" or "What's in it for me?"

Why people raise this: Most probably this will be because they're very busy and they have not understood your purpose or the benefits of getting this job done.

How you can respond: You can try painting a clear picture of how much time it will take and what the personal benefits to them will be. You can talk about the purpose of the work. Then ask them what would make it worthwhile for them. Ask them how much time they could commit. Share your ideas about what they could contribute. Make them feel needed.

"Is it going to be the same old faces?" or "Who else have you asked?"

Why people raise this: They may well be sick of always being asked or of always seeing the same old tired faces producing the same ideas and getting the same results. They may also be worried that there will not be enough people and they will end up with a lot of extra work.

How you can respond: You could talk about whom you have invited and who has already agreed to come. You can share your ideas so far for the kinds of things people will do. They might be interested in what you are doing to invite different people to join you. You could ask for ideas as to who else to invite and what strategy to adopt with them.

"With that many people, why do you need me?" or "If everybody comes, won't you have too many?"

Why people raise this: Some people fear large groups. They get anxious about not being heard or not being able to do anything useful. The concerns range from the fear of being manipulated to the fear of things getting out of control.

How you can respond: Reassurances can help here. You know what you are doing. You need all those people. There will be work for them all. You have planned it all out. Show them the plan. Explain the bits they are concerned about in more detail. Questions can also help. Get their ideas about useful things to do, how to group people, what will be important to make it work.

"I don't know enough to help you" or "Why on earth would you want me?"

Why people raise this: They don't think they have anything to offer, or they don't see the relevance of what they know to what you are talking about.

How you can respond: The best thing here is to get them talking. Give your thoughts and ask questions. Show how much they have to offer by listening to their answers. By drawing them out, as part of the process of inviting them in, you will demonstrate clearly how valuable they can be. It will set the scene for their active involvement.

Following Up

A lot of people will not let you know that they object. Some might not even respond. It's valuable to track the responses. Sometimes the response will be instant and you can immediately proceed to the next step of working with people and planning their involvement in the project. If some people fail to respond, plan a secondary invitation, possibly using a different medium to contact the nonresponders. Otherwise you can begin work as soon as you reach critical mass—that is, as soon as you recruit enough people to get started. Then you might consider a second invitation after you have done some work with the initial group.

You can continue doing follow-up once the work has started. It can be particularly powerful to use your initial volunteers to recruit others. Ask the first few people who accept your invitation to talk to their contacts via phone, in other regular meetings, or by e-mail.

Follow-up needs a high degree of tenacity. When we don't immediately accept an answer of "No"—when we press our case—we convince people we really mean it and we really need them. Sometimes sheer tenacity wins commitment.

Finally, say thank you—and this means to everyone, even those who did not accept your invitation. Who knows? You might be inviting them to join another project soon.

Chapter Checklist

To develop a really special invitation that will draw people into active involvement:

- Review the list of people you want to invite.
- Make notes of what you know or can find out about these people— their needs, interests, and concerns.
- Decide on the most appropriate media for your invitation.
- Prepare a distinctive message for each person you want to invite.
- Respond to objections, track the responses, and follow up as needed.
- Thank everyone involved, including those who turned down your request.

Chapter 4

HOW DO I KEEP PEOPLE INVOLVED?

an Peters had a dream—to bring the 1989 Canadian National Cycling Championships to Ft. McMurray, Alberta.

Ft. McMurray was not really a logical choice for the race. It's a small town in northern Alberta, meaning it would be a long trip for any competitor. The local cycling club had never hosted a major race. Ian's dream was a long shot. He knew it would take a lot of effort to win the bid for the championships and even more to keep people on board for all the planning that would be needed.

Despite these challenges, Ian and his team won the right to host the race. Now they had a new goal: To host the best National Cycling Championships ever.

The Ft. McMurray steering committee went to the 1988 race in Toronto to get a head start on their work. For the next year, the entire committee stayed deeply involved in planning and staging the race. No one left the group. They met regularly to stay on track with time lines. They got together informally in small groups to problem solve over coffee. They traded late night phone calls to celebrate successes and share frustrations.

In the end, they realized their vision. Riders, coaches, fans, and the national governing bodies hailed the Ft. McMurray race as the most successful ever.

Unfortunately, not all stories of involving others go as smoothly as Ian's. It's often frustrating after getting off to a solid start to see progress dissipate over time. Many people find it easier to brainstorm plans than to do the heavy lifting required to implement them. When work becomes hard or boring, it's tough to keep people's attention. Attendance slowly dips at committee working sessions. Or maybe people still show up for weekly meetings, but the mood becomes one of detachment rather than engagement. You find yourself longing for the debates and disagreements that peppered your earlier get-togethers.

Often the same few folks end up doing more than their fair share to get the job done. Well-intentioned teammates miss a conference call or two because of other pressing commitments. You end up as one of only two parents joining your child's overnight end-of-year camping trip when you were positive five hands were raised when the teacher asked for volunteers during the Open House in September. The stories go on and on.

Sometimes these gaps in involvement mean you and others need to pick up the slack and work late or on weekends to get things done. In other situations, you may need to ratchet back your expectations on what you can accomplish. Another option is to concede and wave a white flag: A good idea never becomes reality because you can't keep enough people involved to make it happen.

These bad stories look even worse when you begin calculating the up-front hours spent involving people when you could have dedicated that time to putting your shoulder to the wheel and getting the job done. You've made less progress by involving more people—a convincing case for the anti-involvement people.

This step is about making sure these scenarios aren't part of your story of involving others. It's about working with people in ways that are fun, engaging, and successful—about bridging the gap between making plans and achieving results.

When things are clicking in this step, people work from their strengths, excited to be part of the team. Plans are clear and progress gets made. No matter how busy they may be, people find time to contribute. Instead of shying away from tough challenges, they embrace them. The work draws people in. You don't have to force them to participate—they want to stay involved.

How do you make this happen? The keys are:

- Remind people why they got involved in the first place.
- Keep the key people involved.
- Support people so they want to stay involved.
- Keep an open mind about who stays involved.
- Don't worry if a few team members choose to opt out.

Remind People Why They Got Involved in the First Place

Look for opportunities to remind people about the larger purpose of the work they're doing. When you are buried in daily to do's, it's easy to lose the meaning of the work. To prevent this, help your team tap back into their original hopes and dreams. Talk with them about the progress being made toward your vision. Get back in touch with the enthusiasm you all felt when you first got started. It's easy to stay involved when you are enthusiastic.

When people stay involved, an organization or community can build plans on a longer time frame. Freed from the burden of having to finish projects quickly, groups no longer have to "think small" when "thinking big" is what's needed.

Here's an example. The Performance Network was a small community theatre in Ann Arbor, Michigan. It produced a variety of plays on minimal budgets with amateur actors and operated out of a cramped warehouse with a pole in the middle of the seating area.

One day, the board and staff of the theatre decided it was time to think big. They put together a ten-year strategic plan to transform the theatre. During the next decade, through the ongoing work of scores of people who continually connected back to this original vision, the transformation they envisioned unfolded. Today The Performance Network has become the only professional theatre in Ann Arbor. Housed in a beautiful new play space, the company has won many regional awards for the quality of its productions, even earning national acclaim from playwrights and critics. These results could never have been achieved in the short term nor if people had not been reminded why they chose to get involved in the first place. The only way was through the sustained effort of many people over a long period of time.

That's the power of keeping people involved.

Keep the Key People Involved

Regularly reassess your needs for involving others in what you're up to. Because certain people were helpful as you launched your efforts is no guarantee that they're the right ones to help you complete them. How many times do people feel forced to sit through meetings when they have nothing to offer? In their minds, they have made their most valuable contributions but keep getting notices of the next meeting, keep receiving minutes from the last one. Well-intentioned invitations to keep these folks involved leave them feeling there is no way out of this never-ending cycle.

A surefire way to keep people involved over time is for them to do work that is needed. Involvement gets a bad name when it becomes involvement for involvement's sake. When we're doing work that matters, it's easy to stay involved. When we're contributing from our unique abilities, we stay engaged. Here's a tool (Figure 4.1) you can use to make good decisions about whom to keep involved in your work.

When you continue involving the right people over time, you will make better decisions and get the work done faster. If you get stuck along the way, you can draw on their perspectives and it'll be easier to come up with innovative solutions.

What do you do about those folks whose help you no longer need? First, pause and reflect on the value they've added to your efforts. What have you been able to accomplish because they chose to get involved? Get specific. People will appreciate hearing these details when you thank them for their contributions. Reframe what you might feel is an awkward situation of "dis-inviting" into a celebration. Set time aside and bring others together to publicly acknowledge those who have helped advance the work so far. Often at the same time we're worrying about how to ask someone to no longer be involved, they're wishing they had an elegant exit strategy in hand.

FIGURE 4.1

THE KEEPING THE RIGHT PEOPLE INVOLVED TOOL

Ask yourself the following questions to get clear whom you need to keep involved in your work over time:

- What things do I still need to get done given where I am with this work right now?

- How many people do I need to complete each of these to do's that are now on my list?

- What knowledge, skills, and experience will they need to get these jobs done well?

- Who is already involved that I need to keep involved?

- Who has been involved in the work so far that I don't need to continue involving in the future?

- Who else do I need to recruit to join our team to finish the work?

If you ever do find yourself with someone who wants to continue participating past the point of their being useful to the team, you need to be clear with them. Thank them and explain why you don't believe they'll be able to add value in the work ahead. If they can convince you otherwise, you have just recruited one very committed player for the future. If they can't, stand firm and be prepared to carry on without them.

Support People So They Want to Stay Involved

The most important point to remember about the support you offer others is that they should experience it as supportive. You get no credit for anything else. People don't want to stay involved in work where they don't feel supported. The best way to find out what people will experience as supportive is to ask them. You probably won't be able to respond to every request you receive. Don't worry about that or shy away from asking because of it. For most folks it may be the first time anyone has asked them this question, so you'll be getting a "kid in a candy store" answer. That's okay. Identify a few key items on the list that you can provide immediately. Make a list of others you can go to work on. Also be honest early on and let people know anything that you see as out of reach. All of these strategies will help your team move forward. It will also help you earn your team's trust and respect.

People are seldom provided the emotional support they need to stay involved with efforts over the longer haul. Work becomes a series of tasks to complete instead of something people have passion for and commitment to. You can make sure this does not happen to you by learning why people care about the work they are doing. Take time to talk together about what would happen if you fell short of the mark. What is it about this particular project or initiative that captures their imagination? Why do they believe they're the right people to be doing this work? These questions start conversations, and conversations are good. They breathe life into the purpose, visions, and goals you developed in your planning.

Listen to what people say and, just as importantly, for what they *aren't* saying. Speak your truth about your hopes and fears, and create a safe place for others to do the same. These dialogues will leave you more invested in each other and the work you are doing together.

People also feel supported when we celebrate their accomplishments. Celebrations are often withheld until the end of a project or forgotten altogether. Don't make this mistake. Plan a few interim parties. Take an afternoon off; pick up the tab for a team lunch; take everybody bowling or dancing. The more you surprise people with how you're celebrating, the more they'll want to stay involved with you and the work.

There is a teacher in the Ann Arbor, Michigan, school district who conducts class as if her students were attending Hogwarts School of Witchcraft and Wizardry from the celebrated Harry Potter books. Each day is one celebration after another for the kids. Her students are so involved in their learning that they earned the highest scores for their age level on the annual statewide tests. Have fun pushing your organization's boundaries in celebrating your team's successes.

Keep an Open Mind About Who Stays Involved

People sometimes ask us what to do with troublemakers. This is a critical issue since the effective involver needs to manage the tension between keeping troublemakers involved *and* keeping those struggling with the troublemaker on board at the same time. The initial answer about what to do with troublemakers is, "Welcome them and treat them as your friends." This means putting yourself in the troublemaker's shoes and understanding why you interpret his behavior as troublesome.

The effective involver knows that troublemaking is in the eye of the beholder. Most people (unconsciously) judge their own behavior by different standards than they apply to others:

- "I am a realist, but you are cynical."
- "I am providing needed information, but you talk too long."
- "I stick to my principles, but you are obstinate."

One result is the tendency to label others as troublemakers, even when what they do is not much different from what we would do if we were in their shoes. Instead, try to understand the world from their point of view. This means suspending your natural desire to convince the troublemaker of the rightness of your position and listening—*really listening*—to their point of view.

When you meet up with a troublemaker, start by giving the trouble-maker the benefit of the doubt. If the troublemaker is a "real" trouble-maker, there will be plenty of time to do what happens all too often: ignore them, appease them, punish them, or otherwise make them irrelevant.

Pay attention to what about the troublemaker is getting a rise out of you and others in the group. Do you want to get on with the work at hand and feel like the troublemaker is dragging you down with questions, con-cerns, or resistance? Is it possible you might be trying to work too fast? Do you find yourself in a constant series of arguments with your troublemaker over substantive issues related to the work? Could you have locked in too early on your positions and be blind to new information that could influ-ence your decision? If you assume your troublemaker has value to add to the work you are doing, what might that value be?

Set limits with your troublemaker about the what, when, where, and how long for any conversation. This puts a fence around the conversa-tion, making it safer for both of you. In a group, troublemakers will often say, "Everyone here feels this way" so they appear to be representing the group when they may be just speaking for themselves. Ask the rest of the group, "Who else feels this way?" This allows you to check out whether or not the troublemakers are speaking for themselves or if they truly are representing the group's opinion. It also helps to be explicit about the trouble *you* are having with the troublemaker's behavior. Talk about the troublemaker's behavior and its impact on you. Make specific requests for different behavior.

What do you do when none of this seems to work? Excuse them from further involvement. When you ask a troublemaker to no longer be involved in the work you are doing, you send a message that those who have trouble working well with your team don't belong on it. In the short term, this may lead to more productive and amicable meetings. In the long run, you'll be compromising the creativity and commitment you can count on from reformed troublemakers. Before you lose these valuable contributions, reach out one more time and see your troublemaker as your best friend.

Don't Worry If a Few Team Members Choose to Opt Out

Even if you do everything in your power to keep others involved, you may lose a few recruits. If someone is determined to end their involvement, let them go with thanks for their past efforts. Spending lots of time trying to cajole them to stay will only make you frustrated and them feel defensive.

If people aren't free to leave something you've involved them in—no strings of guilt attached—then others won't feel free to join you. Instead of involvement, you've created a form of coercion. Trust the process when a team member asks to opt out. Believe in an abundant world. There's another fresh-faced recruit around every corner. Celebrate someone's departure as we talked about earlier. Learn from them what made for the best aspects of their being involved with you in this work. What was most difficult? Take what you gather from these "exit interviews" and apply the lessons to the work ahead. If you focus on the benefits of having people involved, you'll begin getting a good reputation in the organization or around town as someone people will want to get involved with. And that's a great way to keep people involved.

Chapter Checklist

The best ways to keep people involved are:

- Remind them why they got involved in the first place.
- Keep those people involved over time that you need involved over time.
- Support people so they want to stay involved.
- Stay open to who stays involved ("troublemakers" can be your best friends).
- Don't worry if a few team members choose to opt out.

Chapter 5

HOW DO I FINISH THE JOB?

At the end of a movie, most people get up and leave while the final credits roll. It's different, of course, if you worked on the movie or know someone who did; if your spouse or best friend was "Third Assistant Gaffer," "Foley Artist," or "Best Boy," you'll stay an extra five minutes for the fun of seeing their name scroll by. When you do, you'll be amazed by the long list of people who get mentioned by name. It takes the combined efforts of thousands of people to make a Hollywood production take shape.

In general, the arts do endings wonderfully well. In the theatre, the actors take a bow as the audience applauds. On opening night or at the end of a long run, the cast throws a celebratory party. At a concert, the musicians perform an encore as a way of giving the audience a little something extra—a special thank you for an appreciative crowd.

There is more to endings than final credits, standing ovations, and parties. We need to let people know the work is completed. We want to leave them ready to join us again. We have lessons we can share that will help us and them do a better job in the future.

If you question the need for a definitive ending, think about the times you were involved in something that just seemed to fizzle out. You may have been unsure whether you were still involved. You may have kept dates free in your diary only to find out later that the work was all over. When our efforts end with a whimper, we feel somehow cheated, as though the whole thing was less than worthwhile. It could easily make us cynical about future work.

One reason that endings matter is that they are opportunities to bring everyone and everything together. They matter because they make things complete. In the midst of any work, things get messy. You may lose track of who is doing what; you may lose sight of how far you have come. At the end, you can stand back from the work and look at it as a whole, reviewing what you've accomplished and how you worked together.

Finally, as with movie credits, the ending of your project expresses the appreciation of the organization or community for everyone who invested their time and energy. It's a significant reward in itself just to have your part publicly acknowledged and celebrated.

In answering the question, "How do I finish the job?" we focus on three things:

- Making sure the job is completed
- Preparing for future work
- Inspiring people to get involved again

Making Sure the Job Is Completed

A final meeting of those involved can help ensure that the job is completed. People can draw together the loose ends, making certain that any handover is clear and that the work is all done. This work can be done face-to-face or virtually. We've conducted some very successful endings using telephone conferences and web-based or e-mail discussions.

Final get-togethers can have the quality of a rite of passage. We all know those important events in our lives when we transit from one stage to another: a marriage, a funeral, a baptism, a bar mitzvah, a graduation. At the ending of involvement, we need to let go and move on. This often requires a ritual.

Ritual can express how we feel and help us to change. It can be highly symbolic or very simple. We might recognize simple ending rituals such as clocking or signing out at the end of a workday. (We probably all remember Fred Flintstone's dramatic daily ending ritual, punctuated with the cry of "Yabadabadoo!") Most people have been to a TGIF party to ritualize the end of a workweek at least once. Actions like this help us deal with the ambiguities of endings. We are both relieved and grieved to see things end.

The art of a final gathering is to combine a review of the work with the symbolism of ritual. Share stories and look for connections and patterns. Look at the events in chronological order, considering similarities and differences in people's experience of the events. Identify what was done well. Discuss what still needs to be done. Hand over outstanding and emerging work to new people. Honor people for the contribution they have made.

People need to be welcomed for a final time. It's often a poignant moment. Set the scene creatively as you did for the first gathering, creating an environment where people can be honest, nondefensive, and celebratory about the work they have done together.

Start off with simple reflections; for example, you might ask people to describe the high points and low points of the project or the funniest moment. People connect with each other quickly as they share their experiences. One ritual you can use here is to ask people to bring something that symbolizes being involved in this work.

The blueprint for meetings throughout the work makes space to look at how things are. In this closing, look backward at the ways things have been and around you at the way they are now as a result of your work. To build up a common picture, share stories in detail and make connections among them. You'll find that almost everyone in the room will learn new things about the work and what happened as it unfolded. This can be a powerful experience, especially when the team had become a community with strong mutual attachments.

A bank had conducted several reengineering projects simultaneously. When nearly all the projects were completed, they gathered the participants to identify what worked well and what they could do differently in the future. What made the meeting particularly rich was the fact that different reengineering approaches had been used in different projects. When the participants reviewed the projects, they not only brought closure to the work, they were able to learn from each other so that future projects could go more smoothly.

Key events can be acknowledged by all and ritually honored for their value. Look beneath the facts. List the key events and facts, and then unpack them. Try to make sense of why things happened that way. What assumptions did you make, and how did these affect people? What kinds of unintended things happened? Use this as an opportunity to talk with other people to see if they had the same experience as you.

Discuss what still needs to be done. Not everything ends. Often the work just moves to a new phase with new people. The work could be ongoing and you may involve different people all the time. Yet for those who are leaving, this is a form of ending. There is a sense of "handing over the baton" to a new team. Give advice to those who will be involved in doing it. Allow those who have been involved to let go and hand over to someone else.

Sometimes there is no clear ending. The work just fizzles out. Maybe no one told us it has ended. Or maybe people stopped being involved without telling us. An example of something fizzling out is a couples group that met for twenty years. They raised their children together and met for rituals and holidays. After twenty years, when the children had left home, people dropped out. Finally they called the group together to ask what people wanted. They found that the group had outlived its usefulness and ended for most. They made sure the work was completed and moved on to other things.

Even the simplest of shared work can have its ritual final gathering. There may only be two of you. You might only talk on the phone the day after you are done. That conversation can include the space to deal with the difficulties of working together, the value of both contributions, and any lessons for involving each other in the future. It can be well worth developing your own ritual for doing this. Include things you like to reflect on and talk about those things that will help you to be better at involving others next time.

Preparing for Future Work

When we finish a job, we would like to leave people better prepared to be involved and involve others in the future, whether it is similar work or something completely different. It can take time and energy to do this. At the end of the work, it might seem easy to think we don't need to invest any more in reviewing what we did. In fact, we might want to avoid going over the difficulties.

Next time we come to do something, we may wish we had captured the lessons and noted ideas for the future. And by then it might be too late. People will have moved on, forgotten a lot of what happened. Lessons will be lost forever.

Building in time at the end for reflection and learning can be invaluable. It can help you with answers to the questions in this book about effectively involving people. It can help you improve your individual ability to contribute. Collective reflection can help a whole team learn how to work together better and improve their products and services.

Reflection and learning needs a deliberate decision to take a step back and look at the connections and patterns in what we have done. When we reflect, we slow down our thinking and consider what we did and why. We notice what assumptions we made about other people. We consider how we reacted to what they did.

People can do this individually. It can be part of the final gathering. It can be written up as a report.

The U.S. Army has developed a disciplined method for doing this; they call it the After Action Review (AAR). After any combat mission or exercise, all the observers and participants gather to share and compare their versions of what happened and identify potential operational improvements.

To start preparing for future work, think about your own effective involvement. If you were the leader, take the time now to look back on the entire process. Think about the people you invited to join you; the way people responded to your invitation; the commitment generated during the planning work; the way involvement grew and developed as the work was done.

Learn something about yourself. Think back to your experience of the project. When were you energized and excited? What was happening at those times? What created the climate for you to feel that way? The answers to these questions can tell you a lot about what you value, how you like to work, and the kind of environment that makes you productive and satisfied.

Here are some of the questions we find useful when reflecting on our work:

- What did we plan for? How did what happened differ from our plans?
- Did we achieve our goals? What else did we achieve that we didn't anticipate?
- Why do we think things developed the way they did? ·
- What do we remember as the key events?
- What assumptions did we make about ourselves and about other people? How did those assumptions prove to be accurate or inaccurate?
- What have we learned as a result of this project?

You can organize your answers to these questions by using the Reflection Tool in Figure 5.1.

FIGURE 5.1

THE REFLECTION TOOL

What did we plan for?	What happened?	Why did it happen?	What were the key events?	What assumptions did we make?	What have we learned?

Have everybody reflect on the same questions. As you and your team members consider these questions, you will build up a collection of fascinating stories about the meaning of the project. Although the stories will have many similarities, they will have differences as well. No two people will remember the events of the project in exactly the same way. That's fine, of course.

One thing we can be sure of. Everyone will have experienced things differently. They will have made different assumptions and reacted to different things. Sharing these at the end of working together can be very powerful. As we publicly share these assumptions and beliefs we learn a lot about ourselves. We also create a common understanding of what makes things work and what gets in the way. We create the opportunity to be better at involving others in the future.

You may want to capture your lessons in a final report, with credits to all involved. The next time your organization launches a project, the leaders will want to study your report and build on the insights it offers.

Don't be too hard on anyone (including yourself) when developing a final report. If you're a perfectionist, you play an important role in your group: You set high standards and push people to achieve them. But be a realist, too. Expect some glitches in any work, and don't beat people up too much about them.

Avoid blame. Someone once said to Julie after she was involved with something that went badly, "You are not to blame, but you are responsible for your own contribution." It sounded a little crazy at the time—but it makes sense. Take an honest look at what happened, including any mistakes you made, and without "blaming" yourself or anyone else, try to see what you did to contribute to those mistakes.

Be nondefensive in making your plans for the future. Avoid apologizing, justifying, or defending yourself. Stand by what you've done and be positive about what you will and will not do in the future.

Remember, even tragedies have an ending. Whatever happened in your project, you need to create closure for yourself and the other people involved. When disappointments fester, the opportunity for learning is lost and you become more likely to repeat your mistakes.

Inspiring People to Get Involved Again

Endings and beginnings are significant transitions. You started your work with a powerful and inspiring invitation. It is equally important to end with something memorable. In the middle of the work, things may have been frazzled. When we are under pressure, we say things and act in ways we later regret. Any bad feelings may leave us not wanting to ever get involved again. An inspiring ending can give us the opportunity to recover some of this.

The art is in bringing closure to the work in a way that celebrates our efforts and achievements. We are not talking about hokey celebrations that embarrass people. Every type of work has its own acceptable ways of celebrating at the end. We have already seen how the movies do it.

You can use the goals you developed at the start of the work as the basis for celebration. You may want to give out Oscar-style awards for achievement of some of the important goals. The awards may be serious or comic. One group gave out awards in the form of weird or surprising presents. The award for "Most Humility" took the form of a hula hoop. When the presenter awkwardly tried to spin the hoop on his hips, the group exploded in laughter.

The last few moments of the final gathering should be memorable. People will say their goodbyes and perhaps make a final gesture of celebration for their achievements. Choose a gesture that fits the mood and style of your team. We've seen groups spontaneously join in a circle and sing. We've seen others bring in percussion instruments (drums, bells, maracas) for everyone to play. Other teams drop balloons, toast themselves with beer or wine, or distribute party favors.

After one weeklong workshop involving fifty people from five organizations—a week full of highs and lows—we gathered around the meeting table for one last time. Each participant took a piece of paper, wrote his or her name at the top of it, and passed the paper to the right. The papers traveled around the circle, each person adding a note of appreciation about the person whose name appeared at the top. In a few minutes, everyone at the table received a wonderful list of inspiring acknowledgments of their contribution to the group.

Chapter Checklist

To finish your job of effective involvement:

- Leave people knowing the job is completed. This frees them to get started on other work and does not keep them coming when there's little value.
- Draw together the loose ends; ensure that any handover is complete and that the work is all done.
- Leave people better prepared to be involved and involve others in the future.
- Take time out to reflect and conduct after-action reviews. This investment is what supports individual and organizational learning and helps us to be better at involving others in the future.
- Leave people wanting more. They should want to be involved again the next time you or someone else comes knocking.
- Have an inspiring celebration, acknowledge people's contributions, and say thank you.

Chapter 6

MEETINGS: THE INVOLVEMENT EDGE

Most people consider meetings time-wasting, energy-draining, and spirit-sapping. Many of us would rather go to the dentist than attend another meeting. Nearly everyone complains about meetings. Most of us seek to reduce the pain by avoiding them or eliminating them—thus dealing with the symptoms, not the problem.

Meetings are miniature involvement processes and as such have highly symbolic value above and beyond the purpose they are called for. It is in meetings where people directly experience involvement. It is here that they learn where the work is headed, decide if the work is worth doing, and find out if their voices count. Low-involvement meetings sap energy while high-involvement meetings produce energy.

Every time we meet represents an opportunity to create and strengthen involvement. In these encounters, people decide whether to remain on board or to walk away, whether to push hard for success or to let things drift, whether to give their all to the project or allow distractions and other commitments to dissipate their energies.

If we want meetings to be dynamic, energy producing, exciting experiences that get things done, then instead of eliminating them we need to focus on making them positive experiences. Instead of working toward reducing the time we spend with each other we need to focus on how to make the time we spend together productive.

A New Blueprint for Meetings

Because we see meetings as involvement opportunities, we look beyond the typical notions of what makes for a good meeting. It's not that agendas and efficient meeting structures aren't important; it's just that we don't think they are enough. Meetings need to be more than something people endure, they need to create energy to get things done.

To help with this task, we have created a meeting blueprint (Figure 6.1). This canoe-shaped blueprint helps create meetings with an "involvement edge." This canoe shape represents the opening up and closing down of a conversation. It is the boat that takes us from the beginning to the end of our time together. When we begin a meeting, the conversation is at its narrowest point. It gradually expands as we develop a clear picture of where we are and where we want to go. It is at this point that the most choices are on the table. The danger at this point is rushing to a conclusion before fully exploring where you are and where you want to go and thereby missing important opportunities. At the same time, you can't explore options forever. The conversation narrows as we make decisions and decide what to do and who does what. Finally, it closes down as we review our decisions and assignments and say goodbye.

Let's explore the elements of our canoe in detail.

FIGURE 6.1

THE MEETING CANOE

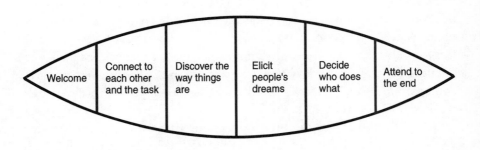

Start by Making People Feel Welcome.   Foyers are designed to help people make the transition from the outside world to the inner world of our homes. In a similar manner, we need to assist people in making a transition from what they have been doing into our meeting. Here are some things to consider that help people feel welcome.

Pay attention to the room. The room sets the stage and influences what happens. Try to work in a room with natural light and plenty of wall space. Make sure everyone can see and hear what's going on; straining to listen drains energy away from the work that needs to be done. And make sure the room is large enough to let everyone breathe.

Pay attention to how people are seated. Seating participants in a circle is usually optimal. The circle represents the most ancient form of interaction as well as a statement of egalitarian spirit. We recommend avoiding hierarchical arrangements, like lining people up in rows or seating them at long rectangular tables. Semicircles work well when the key challenge is to "face the issue." People seated in a semicircle are able to face both one another and the plan that is posted on the wall. We also conduct stand-up meetings occasionally. When people are on their feet, the energy shifts and the mood changes. But stand-up meetings must be short, of course!

Pay attention to how you greet people. Your welcome can be as simple as a handshake or as elaborate as having a string quartet playing to create a mood of harmony and peace. The lobby might feature a simple banner announcing the meeting or a troupe of actors performing mime. Whatever kind of welcome you plan, it should make people feel special as soon as they arrive.

You already know how to make people feel special. You do it in your homes all the time. Think about the last time you had guests for dinner or an overnight stay. You took special care to clean your house beforehand. When your guests arrived, you greeted them in your foyer or on the front porch steps. You offered them tea, coffee, or a snack, as well as a comfortable seat in which to rest their weary bones. Each of these gestures demonstrated that you considered them honored guests, to be treated with dignity, courtesy, and warmth.

Now think back to the most memorable gatherings or social events you've experienced. Chances are good that the welcome you received was something special. We know a company that held a meeting for all its employees to celebrate an important new business initiative. To set the tone, the meeting planners constructed a tunnel for people to walk through as they entered the meeting. The walls of the tunnel were decorated with pictures depicting the company's history from its founding to the present day. What a remarkable way to send the message "Our company is a unique and wonderful organization—and all of you are an important part of it."

Find Ways to Create Connections Among People.   In the words of a saying coined by the faculty of the School for Applied Leadership, "Connection before content." In other words, before people can work together, they must feel connected.

Seeking connections is as natural as breathing. We do it whenever we meet someone new: "Where were you born? Where did you go to school? Do you know so-and-so?" We search for what we have in common so that we can feel more comfortable together. Finding something in common relaxes us and begins the process of transforming strangers into colleagues, partners, and friends.

Conversations help us connect. Some groups we know start their meetings by asking everyone, "What do you need to say in order to be fully present at this meeting?" A quick once around the room with everyone providing a response allows people to "clear their minds" and they are able to bring their whole selves to the gathering.

Personal questions are powerful ways to deepen our connections. They make us uncomfortable, and they make us think. We use questions such as, "Why did you come to this meeting? Why are you staying?" "What are you willing to do to contribute to the success of this meeting? What are you not willing to do?" "What acts of courage will our work require of us?"

As important as it is to connect with others in the room, it is also important to connect to the purpose, our reason for coming together. A common frustration experienced by meeting planners is to bring people together, make a presentation on the importance of what needs to be done, and then be met by silence.

Here is a pattern we frequently observe that we believe is at the root of the problem. The presenter will spend fifty-five minutes of the one-hour meeting making a presentation about why the topic is important. With five minutes to go the presenter will ask if there are any questions. Not wanting to be the only person who stands between the group and getting out of the meeting on time, no one dares raise their hand.

We suggest reallocating time by taking no more than twenty minutes to present information and then using the remaining amount of time for question and answer and discussion. Before starting a question-and-answer session, have people discuss their questions together first. This process of reflecting with others before asking produces better questions and helps the process go smoothly.

Reflecting first can also be used to stimulate discussion. After making a presentation, you can ask those present to reflect together on what interests them about what you have said, what they want to know more about.

When making presentations, avoid death by PowerPoint. A presentation using PowerPoint slides can be a powerful way of conveying information visually. But sitting in the dark looking at images on a screen encourages passivity. Use PowerPoint sparingly and keep it interesting.

Discover the Way Things Are—Build a Shared Picture of the Current Situation.   A common concern we hear is, if we bring different people together the meeting will degenerate into a shouting match with everyone advocating their point of view, not listening to or incorporating others' views. That is because leaders see things one way, followers another. Customers or clients have their own perspective. Outsiders such as neighbors or members of competing organizations have yet another view.

The easiest way to get started building this baseline is to ask people to explain to each other how they do their job. Individual answers will teach everyone about the challenges they meet on a daily basis. Taken together, they'll reveal how the whole system operates. When people understand how the whole system operates, they become more willing to develop solutions that support the whole system operating effectively.

Suppose you are working with your school's Parent-Teacher Association (PTA) to improve the nutritional content of the food served in the cafeteria. You might start your search for common understanding by asking the various people involved in the issue to talk about it from their perspective. The cooks might talk about the limited supplies they have to work with and the time pressures they are under. The school administrators might talk about federal guidelines that have to be met and the budget constraints they are under. The parents might be worried about the fat, salt, and sugar content in the food, without which the students might complain that the food is boring. Each of these perspectives represents a piece of a puzzle. Put them all together and you get the whole picture that needs to be examined if meaningful solutions are to be found.

Another approach is to foster curiosity by asking people to break down and reassemble ideas. For example, a group studied the systems in a hospital by designating one person as a patient. Wearing a sandwich board, this patient traveled from table to table, each table representing a different hospital procedure. At each table, participants wrote a description of what they would do to the patient and posted it on the sandwich board. By the end of the activity, the notes on the sandwich board represented the full patient experience as defined by the entire group.

Another approach is to help people discover what they already know. During a company meeting at a firm that needed to reshape its corporate culture, we asked people to describe their first day on the job. As people told their stories, they uncovered the history of the organization, teaching one another how things came to be.

The previously mentioned approaches support people sharing issues and ideas with people they usually don't talk to. This means creating conversations that cross traditional boundaries—managers talking with employees, the sales department talking with manufacturing, and townspeople talking with the plant manager. It means teachers, parents, and students talking together about curriculum issues. It means doctors, nurses, patients, and insurance company executives talking together about the quality of health care.

When people come together to share their views of the world in this way, the lights go on.

Elicit People's Dreams—Build a Shared Picture of Where You Want to Go.   Have you ever noticed that when you decide that you want to buy a new car you begin to see that car everywhere? Having a clear picture of the current situation (you need a new car), and a clear picture of where you want to go (own a new car), your brain lets in new information. Now those cars were always out there, but because you've established a clear picture of the future you want to create your brain begins to see possibilities you didn't see before.

We've found the arts to be powerful tools for creating a picture of where people want to go. Artistic talent isn't required—just the willingness to share a personal vision of the future.

For example, you might invite the members of your team to make simple drawings that capture an aspect of the future they dream of. Even crude sketches can carry powerful messages about the future.

Sometimes we ask people to create short skits that show them five years in the future. As they act out the future, they show us how things could be, giving life to their imaginations.

Creating "living sculptures" is another approach. Once when we were working with a group of people in the midst of creating a new organization, we asked them to *become* the organization chart, standing in the groupings called for. As the new organizational arrangements came to life, the team members discovered what they liked and didn't like about their plans for the future.

Writing can also be used to uncover the future. Try asking people to imagine themselves five years in the future and spend just five minutes writing about what they see in a free-flowing, open-ended style. The insights that emerge may surprise you.

Perhaps you're dubious about using the arts in this way. We've found that most people are willing to participate in exercises like these as long as they understand that artistic talent is not required. The secret is to say, "This is not about art. We are not here to judge the final results. We want to use drawing [or skits, or writing] as a way of uncovering the future."

If you still shy away from the artistic approach, try simple conversation. Invite people to pretend it is five years from today. Ask them to discuss what they are doing, how they are working together, what their new workplace, church, school, or community looks like. The key is to conduct the conversation in the present tense, as if the future is now—discussing not how you would like it to be, but rather how it "is."

Many varied observations will emerge from this discussion, but in time some common themes will emerge. These themes represent the shared picture of the future—the goal toward which your work will be directed.

Encourage creativity as you build your shared pictures of where you are and where you want to go. We do this through a variety of methods. Exaggeration is one of them. For example, when working to improve the supply chain at an Air Force base, we asked participants to identify how they could *sabotage* the process. Exploring how to make the process fail provided ideas for what was needed to make the supply chain project a success.

Another approach is "single concept thinking." In designing new organizations, we often ask participants to design the organization based on a single criterion such as customer service or quality. In this way, participants are able to delve deeply into that variable without worrying about other constraints. Later we ask people to integrate the best ideas from each category of single concept thinking.

Still another is the concept of an idea fair, in which people visit different booths where ideas are presented. Before leaving each booth, participants jot comments on a sticky note, which gives the idea creators lots of input from a variety of perspectives.

Decide on Who Does What to Create the Future You've Agreed Upon.
Meeting leaders and participants often are frustrated about what happens when they come together to get things done. Instead of leaving with energy and enthusiasm, clear about where they are headed, they often leave confused about future direction. Unclear decision-making processes are often the cause. In order to prevent these negative outcomes there are three things to worry about here: the *how* of the decision, the *what*, and the *who*.

The group must know ahead of time *how* it's going to decide. There are several options. The leader can simply decide; the leader can ask people to offer recommendations and then decide; or the group can make the decision jointly, with everyone having an equal voice. Any of these approaches can be valid. What's most important is that the method you choose is clear and understood by all.

Identifying *what* needs to be done can be handled by simple brainstorming. Sometimes leaders already have an idea of what needs to be done. They can offer their own list as a starting place and ask people to add to or subtract from the list.

In other cases, the group will start from scratch. One technique we've found useful is to have everyone jot ideas of what needs to be done on sticky notes. Post all the notes on an easel or wall, and group similar notes together. Give each grouping a name and identify for each grouping the main task and the subtasks that need to be done.

Another approach is to create a time line on a giant sheet of paper taped to a wall. Invite people to identify what needs to be done and have them jot their ideas on sticky notes. Then have them place each idea on the time line at the point where it needs to be done. In this way a plan will emerge.

Finally, there is the *who*. Again, there are various approaches. The leader can appoint people to be responsible for each task. Volunteers may be called for, perhaps by creating a sign-up sheet. A mixed method is to assign someone to lead a task and then have people volunteer to work on the task.

A more sophisticated version of the sign-up sheet is to identify the *kinds* of people who ought to be involved in a particular task. You can then ask people to volunteer for tasks based on the slots available.

Having identified the *what* and the *who*, it is critical that you review the decisions reached and make sure that everyone understands what has been decided and who is going to do what.

Attend to the End: Pay as Much Attention to Endings as You Do to Beginnings.   Does this sound obvious? Not necessarily. Recently Dick took some lessons in public speaking. At one point, the instructor asked him how he closed his speeches. "I usually end with a question-and-answer session," he replied.

"Absolutely the wrong way to end a speech," the instructor told him. "As the questions and answers gradually peter out, you fade to nothingness. The impact of your speech fades with it."

If you don't want your meetings to end on a whimper, you need to put as much thought and attention into saying goodbye as you did to saying hello.

In our work, we like to end by taking time to review decisions and agreements so that everyone is sure what has been decided and what are the next steps. Then we reflect together on the work that has been accomplished. We ask people to identify what they appreciated about working with others. What helped the work go smoothly? What inspired creativity? Which moments were fun? Sometimes we celebrate our work together with food and drink. We don't rush the ending nor do we drag it out.

Everyone leaves meetings with thoughts about how they could be improved. Why not bring those conversations into your meeting so that you can improve the way you work together? If you end your meetings by asking those present, "What did we do well today and what do we need to do differently next time we meet?" we guarantee that your meetings will improve.

Special Considerations

Large meetings and meetings that extend for more than an hour offer the opportunity to work with groups of various sizes. People sometimes need to work alone, sometimes in pairs, sometimes in small groups, and sometimes in larger groups. Solitude gives people a chance to think things through. Writing or taking a walk are good ways to provide this time for reflection. Working in pairs or trios provides a safe space for people to share ideas. In groups of two or three, people get to know each other in a way that they are not able to do in a larger group. We use large meetings when we want to build a critical mass for change, small groups when we want to develop the details.

Use mixed groups and homogeneous groups as needed. Mixed groups include people with different views or from different parts of the organization. They are important when you want to create innovative solutions or to examine the whole from a variety of viewpoints. Homogeneous groups consist of people with the same point of view. They are valuable when you want to tap into a particular viewpoint. For example, you might have all the supervisors meet together to prepare a report reflecting their perspective on an issue.

Meetings as Rituals

Meetings are stylized rites for coming together. It is in the meeting that the whole system by its behavior demonstrates what's important. Shaking hands, having coffee and donuts, passing out prepared materials for those present, getting the "word" from the leadership, and arranging participants' seating are examples of common meeting rituals.

Long rectangular tables provide structure to a ritualistic way of gathering that emphasizes authoritarian behavior while circular tables emphasize an egalitarian spirit. Handshakes prior to the meeting represent perfunctory connections between people, while taking time to discuss what you have to do or say to be fully present at this meeting allows for deeper connections. Meeting processes that support people discovering what they know naturally and building their future together are powerful involving mechanisms, while being told what to do dampens people's energy.

Over time meeting processes become ritualized. They become the way things are done around here. Recently Dick was in a meeting where the leadership team was discussing an important direction for the company. At one point in the meeting, one of the members said, "I'm not sure why we are discussing whether to adopt this plan; we all know Tom (the CEO) is going ahead with the plan." This group's meeting ritual was that the leader presented a course of action to which he was already committed, the group discussed it for a while, and then when the leader felt he had heard from everybody, he announced his decision, which rarely deviated from his original plan. The group had developed a pseudo-involvement ritual. They went through the motions of involvement while at the same time everyone in the room knew that their voice did not count.

In another organization, the value of connection has become so important that people would not think of beginning their meeting without taking time to welcome newcomers and connect with each other prior to doing the business portion of the meeting. Participants so valued these activities that they have become "ritualized" portions of their meetings.

Rituals help us make meaning of what is going on and build bonds among those present. Some meeting rituals emphasize authoritarian behavior; others emphasize an egalitarian spirit. Most meeting rituals go unnoticed; they are just the way we do things around here. Examining the meaning behind our rituals allows us to uncover hidden messages that may be working for or against the change you are trying to create. When you look for the involvement edge at each stage of the meeting, you create new rituals that add meaning to what you are doing.

Meetings That Generate Involvement

When it comes to meetings, people are constantly making choices. They choose whether and when to show up and whether and when to leave. They choose how much energy they will put forth. They choose to speak up or remain silent. When you understand the power of choice, you conduct your meetings differently. Meetings are rituals that convey powerful messages about how people are going to be involved. Examining our current meeting rituals gives insight into the hidden message behind our actions. Designing meetings using the meeting canoe helps create new rituals that give your meetings the involvement edge.

Is it possible to have a meeting without using the process we've just described? Can you hold gatherings without welcoming people, building connections, building a shared understanding of the way things are, crafting a picture of where you want to go, deciding who does what, and saying goodbye? Of course. But will these gatherings generate the kind of involvement that gets things done? We doubt it.

Chapter Checklist

Here is how you create high-involvement meetings:

- Start by making people feel welcome.
- Take time to foster connections among people.
- Discover the way things are—build a shared picture of the current situation.
- Elicit people's dreams—build a shared picture of where you want to go.
- Decide on who does what to create the future you've agreed upon.
- Pay as much attention to endings as you do to beginnings.

Chapter 7

WHERE TO START

People are always asking us where to start. Here's how some effective involvers we know began their work.

Jan Mears, a human resources director, Global Supply Chain at Kraft, began by taking one of our tools and using it. Upon reading our manuscript Jan used the stakeholder map on page 27 to help her colleagues decide who should be included in a supply chain project.

Keith Smith, a product design manager, as part of a lean engineering process, was asked to figure out how to involve people in redesigning their work area. Keith took a straightforward approach to figuring out whom to include and what kind of involvement was needed. First, he asked the group's supervisor to walk him through the work area. As people explained what they did and how they did it, Keith listened with a different ear. He listened for the people who wanted to improve the way work was done. He then invited those people to join a group charged with the responsibility for redesigning the workflow. Once the group had figured out what needed to be changed, they posted their ideas on easel sheets in the work area and asked their fellow employees to comment. Every day their co-workers put more and more sticky notes on their diagram. The group then reviewed these ideas and incorporated them into the final plan. Within two weeks, the ideas for a more efficient operation were up and running!

Arnold Aprill, director of the Chicago Arts Partnership in Education, a group that incorporates art into the teaching of subjects such as history, math, and science for the Chicago Public Schools, used all the steps as he brought together parents, teachers, students, researchers, marketing experts, and funders to develop a strategic plan.

Repeating Patterns

Change always starts with an individual and the circle then widens to include others. Throughout an involvement process you don't just go through the steps we have described once. You go through them many times.

Consider how the pattern repeated itself at a global manufacturing giant. The work started when the vice president of engineering realized something had to be done about the double-digit attrition rate that was affecting his 23,000-person organization. First, he called together his staff and key union officials to get clear on the work and decide what kind of involvement was needed. Because of the matrix nature of the leadership group, they then involved fifty key leaders in the next step, which was to review the purpose of their work and identify the boundaries of participation. As a result of this meeting, the group refined their purpose to "create a work environment where everyone could be successful."

The group then decided it was time to involve a wider spectrum of employees to set the strategy for going forward. Two hundred fifty people met from all levels and functions along with key union officials. A key question at this meeting was whether the change process should use a waterfall approach, going level by level throughout the organization, or whether the change process should use a ripple strategy, bringing horizontal groups of the organization to decide needed changes. The group said the change strategy should combine the waterfall and ripple approach.

Over the next few months this strategy was implemented as employees came together to carry out the purpose of the work—to create a work environment where people could be successful—and to do it in a way that was consistent with the four principles outlined in Dick Axelrod's earlier book, *Terms of Engagement: Changing the Way We Change Organizations*. These principles are widening the circle of involvement, connecting people with each other, creating communities for action, and embracing democracy.

This work started with one individual answering our questions:

- What kind of involvement is needed?
- How do I know whom to include?
- How do I invite people to become involved?
- How do I keep people involved?
- How do I finish the job?

At each stage of the project from Hank's first meeting, to meetings involving employees throughout the organization, to individual work groups, these questions were answered over and over again at different levels of complexity and different levels of depth by effective involvers throughout the organization.

Three years later, the attrition rate had dropped dramatically; an employee survey indicated a 25 percent increase in employee satisfaction, and when it came time to vote on the union contract, the same group that three years earlier had gone on strike overwhelmingly approved the contract.

Guidelines for Effective Involvers

While each step outlined in this book has its own particular set of ideas, some things are constant in answering every question. We think of them as overriding principles or guidelines. They are worth remembering as you involve others. Here are our guidelines for effective involvement.

Involvement produces results when:

- People believe the job is worth doing.
- People are focused on the task.
- People know that their contributions count.

People Believe the Job Is Worth Doing.   First, the job must be worth doing—not just from the leader's perspective, not just from the follower's perspective, but also from everyone's perspective. When you alone know your reasons for getting something done, you become a used car salesman, selling a broken-down jalopy to someone who can't drive. Have you ever tried to sell something that no one wants? It takes a lot of effort and rarely works. But when you know what needs to be done from everyone's perspective, you become a salesperson in the best sense of the word, delivering a product that everyone wants.

We answer the question, "Is this job worth doing?" when we get clear on the work and decide what kind of involvement is needed. We tap into the power of this question in the invitation and get people thinking about it whenever we meet. Discussing questions such as, "What do we want to create?" and "What do we want to be different as a result of our work together?" helps us decide that the job is worth doing.

The key to these discussions is for people to identify why the project is important to the organization, their group, and most importantly, to them.

Check:

✓ Why is it important?

✓ Who cares?

✓ Will it make a difference?

People Are Focused on the Task. Second, the task must be focused. Focus occurs when you know where you are headed, how you will get there, and what is expected of you. To help people stay focused on the task, revisit your goals and your progress toward them frequently.

All this works better when people are involved from the start in deciding where they are headed, how they will get there, and what role they will play, as well as doing their own progress checks.

Having a clear purpose, knowing your boundaries before you start, thinking through who needs to be included to get the job done, identifying the current state of affairs and what you want to achieve—all these processes help you maintain focus.

Check:

✓ Where are we headed?

✓ How will we get there?

✓ What do we expect of each other?

People Know That Their Contributions Count.   Finally, people must know that showing up matters, that their contributions count. When you know your contributions are valued, you put forth more effort and take responsibility for making sure the job is done right. People know that their contributions matter when their voices are heard and their ideas are considered. This does not mean that you have to get your way; rather it means that you are listened to, you are understood, and you can see how your ideas contributed to the outcome.

Recently at a large group meeting to redesign the supply chain at Detroit Edison, an electrician got up at the end of the meeting and said the following: "We're always saying, how come they don't ask me? I do the job. I'm involved with it. Someone is always making decisions for me. Now I feel that they did ask us. We gave our input. Let's see if we know what we're talking about."

A press operator at R.R. Donnelley and Sons, Inc., said the following when asked about his involvement in the redesign of the plant: "Even if you didn't agree with what was said, it made you think."

Clearly both the electrician and pressman knew that they had been listened to and that their contributions counted.

Check:

✓ Do people feel understood?

✓ Are people's contributions recognized?

✓ Are people's contributions connected to the outcomes?

Many Ways to Start

Another question people often ask us is, "Can I only use these ideas when I'm starting my work?" Because involvement is a repeating pattern you can start anywhere. You can start with an ending, you can start with a beginning, or you can start somewhere in between. There are a number of ways to start. Here are some examples:

- Start with yourself by going through the steps outlined in this book and see where that leads you. You can use the tools contained throughout the book to help you decide how to involve others. Once you have done this on your own, you may want to share your thinking with others.
- Start with a question that is troubling you by picking one of our five questions and begin there. Suppose you are concerned about whom to include; start by using that chapter to help you decide who needs to be there.
- Start by designing your meetings using the ideas contained in "Meetings: The Involvement Edge." Because meetings are involvement processes in miniature, they present a powerful opportunity to shift how you involve others. Use our meeting canoe as a guide to creating high-involvement meetings.
- Discuss our questions with a group that is a representative sample of the people you wish to involve. Use this "kitchen cabinet" to help determine how you will involve others in getting things done. In this way, you involve people from the very beginning.
- Start at the end. If you are at the end of your work you can use our chapter "How Do I Finish the Job?" as a starting place. One organization we know called together everyone who had participated in a strategic planning process to review what they did. Taking the ideas from this chapter, they reviewed what contributed to their success and what they would do differently next time, thus providing the seeds for new and improved ways to include others.

No matter where you start, at the beginning or in the middle, whether you start by reviewing these questions by yourself or with a group, the most important thing is to start. Do something and learn from it.

Appendix a

THE INVOLVEMENT CHECKLIST

Decide what kind of involvement is needed . . .

- Use the Return on Involvement Assessment Tool (Figure 1.1) to think through the risks and rewards of involving others in your work or going it alone.
- Determine if it makes sense to tackle the work in front of you without involving anyone else. If it does, go to it and get the job done.
- If you've gotten clear that you want to include others in your efforts, decide what kind of involvement will be most useful in your particular circumstances:
  - Know-How Involvement
  - Arms and Legs Involvement
  - Caring and Commitment Involvement
  - Teaching and Learning Involvement

Decide whom to include . . .

- Think about whom to include based on the six categories: people who care, people with authority and responsibility, people with information and expertise, people who will be personally affected, people with diverse points of view, and people who are considered troublemakers.
- Brainstorm all the relevant stakeholder groups.
- List the people you must have to succeed and those who would be nice to have to support the work.
- Decide whether you want to open the project up to volunteers, and, if so, how many.
- Chunk out what you see as the stages, and think through the kinds of people you would like to include at each stage.
- Make the final selection of people to invite, basing the number of invitees on the nature of the project and practical considerations such as the amount of time and money available.
- Adjust as you go along.

Create your invitation . . .

- Review the list of people you want to invite.
- Make notes of what you know or can find out about these people—their needs, interests, and concerns.
- Decide on the most appropriate media for your invitation.
- Prepare a distinctive message for each person you want to invite.
- Track the responses and follow up as needed.
- Thank everyone involved, including those who turned down your request.

Keep people involved . . .

- Remind people why they got involved in the first place.
- Keep those people involved over time that you need involved over time.
- Support people so they want to stay involved.
- Stay open to who stays involved.
- Don't worry if a few team members choose to opt out.

Finish the job . . .

- Leave people knowing the job is completed.
- Draw together the loose ends; ensure that any handover is complete and that the work is all done.
- Leave people better prepared to be involved and involve others in the future.
- Leave people wanting more.
- Celebrate and say, "Until we meet again."

Meetings: The Involvement Edge . . .

- Start by making people feel welcome.
- Take time to foster connections among people.
- Discover the way things are—build a shared picture of the current situation.
- Elicit people's dreams—build a shared picture of where you want to go.
- Decide on who does what to create the future you've agreed upon.
- End by saying goodbye.

Things to remember . . .

- Make sure that your project is worth doing, that people are focused on the task, and that people know their contributions count.
- Be aware that you'll go through the same pattern at every stage of the project.
- Start small.
- Don't start unless you plan to finish.

Appendix **b**

FOR FURTHER LEARNING

Richard Beckhard and Rueben T. Harris, *Organizational Transitions: Managing Complex Change*, Addison-Wesley, 1977. A classic, easy-to-understand book on organizational change.

Geoff Bellman, *Getting Things When You Are Not in Charge*, Second Edition, Berrett-Koehler, 2000. When involving people, there are plenty of times when you are not in charge. Geoff's book offers plenty of practical suggestions on how to engage people in work you need to get done.

Peter Block, *The Answer to How Is Yes: Acting On What Matters*, Berrett-Koehler, 2002. Shows that the most pragmatic way to answer questions is to pursue them deeply.

Terrence E. Deal and M. K. Key, Ph.D., *Corporate Celebration: Play, Purpose, and Profit at Work*, Berrett-Koehler, 1998. This practical guide for improving morale and performance examines the importance of celebrations and provides clear guidelines for the design of meaningful, top-flight celebrations.

Roger Fisher, William Ury, and Bruce Patton, *Getting to Yes*, Second Edition, Penguin, 1991. This book is a classic from the Harvard Negotiation Project. We include it here as a primer on how to understand the underlying interests, needs, and wants of folks you'll be including in your projects. If you can't connect with people about what they care about, they won't connect with you about what you care about.

Robert Fritz, *The Path of Least Resistance for Leaders*, Berrett-Koehler, 1999. Shows leaders how, when people understand their current reality and the future they want to create, change happens.

Malcolm Gladwell, *The Tipping Point: How Little Things Can Make a Big Difference*, Little, Brown, 2000. The "connectors," "mavens," and "salesmen" Gladwell describes are an interesting twist for you to consider in thinking through whom to involve in your project work. The book is filled with fascinating stories that bring these concepts to life. You get big things done not just by involving people, but by involving the right kind of people at the right times.

Ron Lippitt and Eva Schindler-Rainman, *Building the Collaborative Community: Mobilizing Citizens for Action*, Riverside Press, University of California, 1980. Seminal thinking on the concept and practice of "preferred futuring" in community settings. Ron and Eva trace its application in more than eighty communities around the world on a wide variety of projects.

Edgar H. Schein, *The Corporate Culture Survival Guide*, Jossey-Bass, 1999. In this most practical of books, Ed Schein unravels the mystery of corporate culture and how to change it. Combine Schein's ideas with pragmatic involvement and you have a dynamite combination.

Douglas Stone, Bruce Patton, and Sheila Heen, *Difficult Conversations: How to Discuss What Matters Most*, Viking, 1999. Built on lessons from *Getting to Yes*, this book zeroes in on how to productively involve others in conversations that are tough and might otherwise be avoided. Effective involvers have to be experts at raising issues without starting a fight, while not ignoring them and paying the price down the line. This book shows you the way out of these dilemmas.

Georg Von Krogh, Kazuo Ichijo, and Ikujiro Nonaka, *Enabling Knowledge Creation: How to Unlock the Mystery of Tacit Knowledge and Release the Power of Innovation*, Oxford University Press, 2000. Tacit Knowledge is the practical how to's that people share with each other. The authors show how to create organizations where knowledge is shared freely.

Marvin Weisbord, *Productive Workplaces: Organizing and Managing for Dignity, Meaning, and Community*, Second Edition, Jossey-Bass, 2004. Marv's book tells the story of involvement. It covers the birth of the field of organization development through to the present day. There's great history here, supplemented by behind-the-scenes stories of the field's giants that shaped thinking and work today.

OTHER BOOKS BY THE AUTHORS

Richard H. Axelrod, *Terms of Engagement: Changing the Way We Change Organizations*, Berrett-Koehler, 2000. If you've ever asked yourself, "How can we get the entire organization to support your change effort?" you are not alone. Here Dick shows why current approaches to change often create resistance instead of reducing it and provides readers with a practical, principle-based strategy for creating successful change outcomes. There are plenty of case studies and lessons applicable to any change project you're undertaking.

Richard H. Axelrod and Emily M. Axelrod, *The Conference Model*, Berrett-Koehler, 1999. In this booklet, Dick and Emily describe their approach to redesigning organizations and processes.

Robert W. Jacobs, *Real Time Strategic Change: Involving an Entire Organization in Fast and Far-Reaching Change*, Berrett-Koehler, 1997. Jake's book describes how to bring large groups of people together to create their future, faster. Chock full of tools and techniques, it walks you through a step-by-step process for unleashing the hearts, minds, and hands of your total organization.

Robert W. Jacobs and Frank McKeown, *Real Time Strategic Change*, Berrett-Koehler, 1999. In this booklet, Jake updates his previous work and provides readers with a condensed version of his original text.

VISTA Consulting Team Limited, *Meetings by Design*, VISTA Consulting Team Limited, 2002. Written by Julie Beedon and her partners in VISTA, this hands-on tool kit is a must for every Pragmatic Involver. It describes a multitude of ways to include others and make meetings something people want to attend instead of the energy-draining punishment we have come to accept as "the way things have to be."

TRAINING BY THE AUTHORS

Having just finished this book, you might be wondering what else is available. Over the years we have developed several different training vehicles. You may well find these useful in making change happen in your organization.

- In-house training
- Off-site retreats
- Keynote speeches
- Public seminars
- E-learning

To learn more about these, contact us at:
info@youdonthavetodoitalone.com, or call us at 877-233-8054.

We'd love to hear about your experiences bringing people together to get things done. Visit us at www.youdonthavetodoitalone.com, and share what you've done.

INDEX

The four authors taking a break from writing. Left to right: David Axelrod (Dick and Emily's son, ski instructor and raft guide extaordinaire), Robert (Jake) Jacobs, Emily Axelrod, Dick Axelrod, Julie Beedon.

ABOUT THE AUTHORS

Richard H. Axelrod is a founder of, and principal in, The Axelrod Group, Inc.—a consulting firm that pioneered the use of employee-involvement to effect large-scale organizational change. He now brings over twenty-five years of consulting and teaching experience to his work, with clients including Boeing, Coca Cola, and Hewlett Packard. Dick received his masters in business administration from the University of Chicago. Raised in Chicago, he is a lifelong Cubs fan.

Emily M. Axelrod is also a founder of, and principal in, The Axelrod Group, Inc., which she created with her husband. For the past twenty-five years, she has consulted to Fortune 500 companies, educational institutions, government agencies, healthcare organizations, and nonprofits. With Southern wit and spirit, she helps build more productive, energized, dignified enterprises. Emily has two master's degrees: one in education from the University of North Carolina and one in social work from Loyola University.

Julie Beedon co-founded VISTA with the aim of "Making a Difference in the World." She does this by engaging organizations and communities to create a desirable future. Julie brings energy, enthusiasm, and a mathematics degree to her work. She loves theories, concepts, and principles, while enjoying a healthy debate about why they work. Julie's clients range in size from small Staffordshire villages in the UK to global multinational organizations such as Royal Dutch Shell.

Robert W. Jacobs is a partner in the change management practice at Mercer Delta Consulting. Jake has a simple philosophy to change: if you think of change work as something special, you'll never get around to doing it. Change work needs to be part of your daily work. In doing so, you begin living your future now. Jake's clients embracing this philosophy include Ford, Marriott, and the City of New York. Jake lives in Los Angeles with his wife, Cheryl; children, Alison and Aaron; and four-legged friends, Chester, Chloe, Madison, and well-trained buddy Theo.